TAROT Secrets

A Fast and Easy Way to Learn a Powerful Ancient Art

Amy Zerner & Monte Farber

The Enchanted World of Amy Zerner & Monte Farber

Tarot Secrets
A Fast and Easy Way to Learn a Powerful Ancient Art

This edition was created for One Spirit® by
Zerner/Farber Editions, Ltd.

For information, address:
The Enchanted World of Amy Zerner & Monte Farber
Post Office Box 2299, East Hampton, NY 11937 USA
E-mail: info@TheEnchantedWorld.com
Website: www.TheEnchantedWorld.com

Library of Congress Cataloging-in-Publication Data
available on request.

ISBN: 978-1-61523-078-5

First U.S. Edition published 2009

9 8 7 6 5 4 3 2 1

Graphic Design by Rose Sheifer-Wright

Printed in China through Colorcraft Ltd, Hong Kong

For entertainment purposes only

one spirit®

CONTENTS

The Magician
ENERGY
21
The World

Introduction

Ever since our ancestors realized that there was such a thing as *the future*, people have explored various ways to predict it. They took this pursuit very seriously. In fact, one of the terms for foretelling the future is *divination*, a word that harkens back to the time when it was thought that the oracle—the person doing the predicting—was getting in touch with the all-knowing Divine. This importance lingers on in the storied practice of reading Tarot cards.

My wife, Amy Zerner, and I take divination seriously because it works for us. As professional readers, we use our Tarot cards to give our clients accurate guidance about past, present, and, yes, even future conditions—information that they can use to make good decisions in their personal lives and careers. Of course, we also read for each other and for our friends and family with similar, positive results.

Back in the day when we used to have our Tarot cards read by other people, every reader told us, "You have the gift—you can read Tarot cards, too!" So we learned how to do it using the books that were available at the time, and though they were quite difficult, we didn't give up. We've done thousands of readings since.

That was more than thirty years ago. Though we are still learning and always will be, those for whom we read Tarot cards tell us that they consider us to be master counselors whose guidance has helped them have better relationships, more success on every level, and even better jobs and places to live. Amy and I have a great life filled with love, light, and laughter. Our ability to read Tarot cards is certainly one of the main secrets of how we've created our enchanted life together.

The main secret we'd like to share with you in *Tarot Secrets* is this: You have the gift—you can read Tarot cards, too! It's true, or else you would not have been guided to this book. Moreover, you have the gift we wish we'd had when we were learning to read Tarot cards, namely *Tarot Secrets* itself. That's why we wrote it, filling its pages with the best techniques we know to get you reading Tarot cards like a pro quickly, easily, and enjoyably.

In our experience, Tarot card reading is not fortune-telling, but it can help you make your fortune. We use Tarot readings as part of our decision-making mix, and this practice has enabled us, our loved ones, and our clients to achieve success in business. To paraphrase legendary financier, banker, and art collector J.P. Morgan's often-quoted statement about the practice of real astrology (in which we are also expert counselors), "Millionaires don't use Tarot cards; billionaires do." We're not billionaires yet, but we're working on it!

Reading Tarot cards is not a fanciful waste of time. Rather, it is a practical skill that can help one be more successful not just financially but on every level of daily life.

Reading Tarot cards is not a fanciful waste of time. Rather, it is a practical skill that can help one be more successful, not just financially but on every level of daily life. In this age of prepackaged mindless electronic infotainment, we have found it to be real entertainment, thought provoking, deeply therapeutic, and spellbinding.

Like the most satisfying entertainment, reading Tarot succeeds because there is a genuine spiritual element to it; it is valuable on all levels of our being. That is why we have devoted our lives to helping people learn to do it for themselves. No matter what your skill level or even your belief in the possibility of foretelling the future, just the practice of trying to derive symbolic meaning from the cards helps you expand your mind to new possibilities and ways of thinking. Even skeptics can have fun with it and may develop a surprising belief once the cards are laid out and the reader—that's you!—begins to interpret their messages.

In the pages of *Tarot Secrets* we have simplified the centuries-old process of reading Tarot cards, updating this powerful ancient art for your twenty-first-century life. Our user-friendly approach to it is to view the practice as a fun and useful tool that can help you find the answers you seek anytime and anywhere.

When you need information, what do you usually do? You ask someone who knows, you look it up in a book or a library's microfilms, or you use a computer to access one of the Internet's many powerful search engines—Google is the one you've probably used or heard about—which enable you to find in seconds what you're looking for.

For centuries Tarot cards were used as an early form of Google. We believe that is the best way to think of them, in other words, as a tool for obtaining information and guidance. A deck of Tarot cards—*your* deck of Tarot cards—can offer a useful and surprisingly accurate picture of present conditions. It can also tell you how the past has brought these conditions into being. In skilled hands (like yours are or soon will be) Tarot cards can even offer useful guidance about the probable conditions that may be encountered in the future.

I don't blame anyone for being skeptical about whether Tarot cards can tell the future. I used to look at Tarot cards, astrology, and the like the same way. When I met my wife and co-collaborator, the artist and fashion designer Amy Zerner, back in 1974, she was studying Tarot and astrology and I was studying Amy, so I learned Tarot and astrology, too. They became our language of love, and we're still going strong.

Back then I thought it was all nonsense. Luckily for me, I fancied myself a logical and scientific kind of guy and I had read a saying by the great scientist Sir Thomas Huxley, who said, "I'm too much a skeptic not to believe that anything is possible." So I gave them a fair and scientific hearing and I was astounded to discover that Tarot cards, astrology, and many other practices labeled "occult" (meaning "obscured or hidden") are in truth useful tools for gaining otherwise unobtainable information about people, places, events, and circumstances unrestricted by location or time! Scientists would make quantum leaps if they started with the assumption that this was true. Actually, quantum physicists are starting to come around to believing this to be the case, so we can expect some amazing inventions in the coming years.

Like scientific research, a Tarot reading's degree of accuracy is dependent on the proficiency of the reader. Fortunately for you (and us), Amy and I are two of the most expert Tarot readers in the world. Our *Enchanted Tarot*, *Instant Tarot Reader*, *Zerner-Farber Tarot Deck*, *True Love Tarot*, and *Tarot Discovery Kit* have sold more than half a million copies in five languages. We have now distilled the essence of our decades of study and practice into the pages of this book so that you can read virtually any seventy-eight-card Tarot deck quickly and easily.

There is something here for everyone who reads Tarot cards or wants to learn how. Whether you need help picking your first deck, are one of the millions of people who have a deck but don't know how to read it, or are an expert reader who wants to add some new ways of looking at the cards to your skill set, *Tarot Secrets* can provide many hours of enjoyable readings for you and those who want you to read their Tarot cards—in other words, almost everyone else you know!

There's nothing to memorize—it's all right here in this book—but after a while you'll be surprised at how much you remember, and you'll consult our way of doing things less often as you formulate your own. *Tarot Secrets* contains insightful interpretations, upright and reversed card meanings, the compelling spiritual journey through the first twenty-two cards of the Tarot (also known as the Major Arcana), and many helpful spread techniques gained from our thirty years of experience of laying out and reading the cards.

You're going to start by doing readings with one card, which is the way most professional readers read for themselves daily to gain insight about simple questions such as "Should I take the bridge or the tunnel?," "Will my guests be here soon?," "Should I read for this person?," or "What is this person's real issue in this situation?" You will be amazed at how one little Tarot card can give you so much information, garnered not just from what's on the printed page but through the intuitive, creative insights that will flow to you, triggered by the card you've drawn.

Tarot Secrets offers a "Quick Read" if you are in a hurry, "Keywords" that trigger intuitive associations, plus the "Secret" of each card, which sums up what you need to know right now. We also provide a longer interpretation of each card so that you can go deeper into the card's archetypal meanings and universal lessons.

But wait—there's more! *Tarot Secrets* also contains twelve Master Spreads—specific diagrams of how to spread out anywhere from three to twelve cards to obtain more detailed guidance about particular types of questions. Simply lay out the cards according to the diagram of your chosen spread, depending on the type of question you have, and then look up the meaning of each card, either upright or reversed.

The Tarot helps you to be more mindful by allowing you to tune in to a deeper, inner level of awareness. It is a way to journey in to yourself and tap into your spiritual center. You may find, as we did, that reading the cards with our time-proven methods seems to subtly alter the way you look at life, especially once you start doing multiple-card spreads.

For some of you, especially those who end up spending years doing readings for others, using the Tarot as a focusing mechanism and benefiting from learning how to think symbolically may even help in the development of your latent psychic abilities. This is what happened to me (Monte). Today I am a professional psychic whose client sessions start with a Tarot reading, just as the development of my psychic gift was facilitated by my years of interpreting the cards. Even so, especially when you are learning, it is a good idea to view your readings as research, not the revealed word of God/Goddess.

A Gentle Warning

The Tarot is not meant to dictate your actions or run your life. Rather than telling you what to do, the cards and various spread techniques offer advice and put you in touch with how you feel about what is going on in your life, thereby helping you to make better decisions. The Tarot spices up your life, but you can't live on spices. Always remember to keep your Tarot readings in perspective. This quote from the Buddha may help you do so:

Believe nothing, no matter where you read it, or who said it, no matter if I have said it, unless it agrees with your own reason and your own common sense.

—Buddha

Even the best and most accurate Tarot readings done by the greatest readers are not a substitute for your own logical thought processes and conventional planning methods or the advice of licensed professionals whom you have thoroughly investigated and found credible. There's no reading so good that it cannot be undone by the free will of the person who received it. Likewise, there's no reading so dire that it cannot be made better by the guidance offered by a follow-up, clarification reading. All you have to do is ask and you shall receive guidance. What you do with the answers you receive is totally up to you.

Where does the information come from? We have included in this book all you need to know to get valuable information from a Tarot card reading, but we firmly believe that, once you get to know the basics of the process, the most important guidance is actually that which comes from your own intuition. We have found this to be the source of the additional insights that are not part of the traditional meaning of the Tarot cards but prove equally useful to our decision-making mix. It is this fact that can develop a reader's psychic abilities.

Using the Tarot as a meditation tool helps you to dialogue with what we call your "Higher Self." In any case, consulting the cards should create for you a safe, spiritual haven where you feel you can connect to positive energy and positive emotions. It is in that space that we can discover what we really want in life and what we must do as our next step on the path to achieving it.

You can use the cards laid out in specific spreads whenever you need clarity on an issue, or as an everyday meditation. When you read your message, you can reflect on your attitudes, desires, and strategies for the best course of action. The process requires opening your mind and trusting your intuition to interpret the answers. It is in this way that the Tarot is a tool that helps you tap into your psychic power.

Intuition is like a muscle and can be made stronger by being properly exercised. The best way to exercise your intuition is to use it consciously. When you learn to use and, most important, trust your intuition, it will keep on getting stronger. We call a person with an extraordinarily developed mind a genius, and we call a person with extraordinarily developed intuition a psychic.

Both of these special groups of people are fairly rare in our society, but their very existence is a reminder of the power of the brain. Scientists seem to be fond of saying how small a percentage of our brain's real abilities and power we actually use. I would like to suggest that one of the reasons studies show this is because a large part of the brain that we are not using is connected with the abilities associated with our intuition. Unless we believe that we even have these abilities, how can we use them? That is why for most people, intuition comes in flashes: hunches, gut feelings, premonitions, or precognitive dreams, when the culturally supported tyranny of our rational mind is absent and our intuition is free to work for us.

Even though most people have these types of intuitive flashes, they usually do not listen to them. How many times have you heard people say they wish they had listened to that little voice inside that was telling them to do or not do something? How many times have you been the person saying that? By learning to read Tarot cards the *Tarot Secrets* way, you are taking an important and powerful step toward fully developing your gifts of intuition. As you keep exercising that gift by reading the Tarot, you will learn to trust it more.

Reading Tarot cards has the added benefit of highlighting forces and influences in your life that might otherwise go unnoticed. Tarot card reading is one of the best ways to gain new perspective and generate creative ideas—and it makes you very popular in social situations, too!

Each Tarot reading can reveal valuable information about a separate adventure on the journey that is your life. By using specific spreads, a reader can gain insight into his or her life path, receive guidance on a course of action, or learn about another person's character and motives. For example, you can make a wish and read the outcome, get a birthday reading that describes your coming year, gain information about relationships and family issues, identify your fears and a path to dealing with them, or discover how to balance your chakras (I'll tell you what that means later).

I once asked Amy, "What do you think is the common denominator of all human-caused suffering?" She replied without hesitation, "Poor decision making." One of the greatest things about reading Tarot cards is that it is an ongoing learning process that is a perfect complement to your daily life. Our *Tarot Secrets* are now in your hands, and if they help you improve your intuition, make better decisions, and enjoy your life more, then we all will have done our jobs well—and had a lot of fun doing it!

Secrets for Choosing Your Tarot Deck

The deck you choose should resonate with you in some way and stimulate your imagination.

Tarot Secrets has been designed to empower you with our quick and easy system for answering any question about your past, your present, or your future using virtually any seventy-eight-card Tarot deck, not just the ones contained in the several book/Tarot deck sets we have created since 1990: *The Enchanted Tarot*, *True Love Tarot*, or our *Zerner-Farber Tarot Deck*, which is contained in both our *Instant Tarot Reader* and *Tarot Discovery Kit*.

Of course, we'd be honored if you chose any of our decks to use as your own. You're going to get to know the cards from our Tarot decks—or to be more precise, Amy Zerner's Tarot decks—because we've used them to illustrate *Tarot Secrets*. Amy is a National Endowment for the Arts award-winning fine artist, and she used her pioneering fabric collage tapestry technique to create each and every one of the gorgeous tapestries that are used as the images on our cards.

I'll tell you a secret: She created the tapestries first, meditating on the meanings of the individual cards as she created them by using fabric the way a painter uses paint. Only after they had been sewn together did I meditate on each completed tapestry and write the meanings I saw in each one—which is the opposite of how decks are usually created. In truth, I "illustrated" her tapestry Tarot cards with my words.

Proud as we are of our "kids," as we call our creations, we are not the only innovative people who have created our very own Tarot decks—far from it! There are several hundred different Tarot decks commercially available today. There are also a large number of decks that were published over the years but have gone out of print. In most cases, these can still be purchased through bookstores that sell used books or through online Web sites such as Barnes & Noble, Amazon, or eBay.

Other great artists—Salvador Dalí is one—have created Tarot decks based on many themes, so many that they are too numerous to mention here. Each deck has its own individual style, design, and feel. Some decks are based on mythological or cultural themes, while others are based on spiritual or philosophical themes. There are, to name just a few, animal, Renaissance, angel, Wiccan, mermaid, Russian, and Celtic themes. There are also quite a few that defy categorization. Using online search engines such as Google, all you have to do is type in "Tarot deck" and then sit back—a virtual torrent of Tarot decks will appear.

You can also buy a blank Tarot deck and make your own illustrations if you are so inclined. Type in "artist create Tarot deck" and you will find many Web sites with advice for creating your own deck. You will also find a few that connect you to artists who can create your own Tarot deck for you.

Some people collect Tarot decks for their artistry alone and never learn to use them for readings. Experienced readers often use particular decks for certain types of readings, such as love, business, or divine guidance. There really is a deck for every person, every purpose, and every taste.

So, what is the secret for choosing the "right" Tarot deck for you? It's the fact that you don't have to know anything about the Tarot to choose your deck of Tarot cards.

You are going to be spending a lot of time looking at your deck, so, for most people, the main requirement is that it be visually appealing. The deck you choose should resonate with you in some way and stimulate your imagination. Are the images well done? Is there something about them that speaks to you, makes you feel inspired and a part of the centuries-old tradition of Tarot readers? When you look at the images, do you find yourself daydreaming? Daydreaming is a good thing when you're trying to listen to your intuition.

To a number of students of the Tarot, however, the look of a deck is not that important. Some want a deck that has existed for a long time, such as the Marseilles deck. Some want a deck associated with an esoteric philosophical tradition, such as the Golden Dawn, the Crowley, or the Rider-Waite deck.

When choosing your deck, please be aware that some decks, such as the old Rider-Waite deck and our *Enchanted Tarot* and *Zerner-Farber Tarot Deck*, use full illustrations for all seventy-eight cards, while others, such as the even older Marseilles deck and our *True Love Tarot*, do not illustrate the ace through ten pip cards, instead rendering them like playing cards: the aces have one symbol, the twos have two symbols, and so on.

The many Tarot decks that have been created in the past few decades, including ours, have taken the basic meanings of these wonderful traditional decks and updated them for our time and tastes. In our case, one of our goals was to take the scariness out of traditional Tarot imagery that had heretofore stopped many people from even considering learning to read Tarot cards.

One of the reasons that Tarot reading was misunderstood during the Dark Ages (and still is by a few people who want to live in the past) is that every Tarot deck has a Death card, which symbolizes change or the end of a process, and a Devil card, which symbolizes the seduction of the material world. Be certain, whichever deck you choose, that you are comfortable with the appearance of these two cards especially, as well as with all the challenging cards in the deck. This is exceptionally important if you intend to use your deck to read for others.

Be reassured: I've gotten the Death card hundreds of times and I'm still here, though I may not be when you're reading this. This book will be in print for a very long time if we successfully navigate the seduction of the material world—the world of business and politics and celebrity—and all artists want their work to survive them. Change, endings, and the seduction of the material world have been around since time began and always will be. Here's a secret I learned from the Death and Devil cards: To be afraid of death is to be afraid of life, and it is the love of money that is the root of all evil, not money itself.

I have just revealed another secret: Learning to read Tarot cards is more than a little like learning philosophy because so many of life's central lessons are contained in the meaning of your Tarot cards.

How do you get to preview the images of the various Tarot decks available before you purchase yours? This brings us to another of the many superstitions associated with the Tarot. Though I can scarcely believe anyone could even dream this up, some people have the notion that tradition says that you should never buy your own deck; someone should buy it for you. Outrageous!

Amy and I have read Tarot cards for decades, and we've sold hundreds of thousands of our own decks, so, not surprisingly, we do not agree. We love gifts, and if someone gives you a Tarot deck, that's great. We've just explained, though, how important it is for you to feel comfortable with the deck you're going to read with. So if you are superstitious, which I am not, then pick out your deck and then ask someone to buy it for you. That sounds to me like too much work, and, besides, do you really want everyone to know you're superstitious? If you want to make magic, then keep what you're doing a secret. You should feel free to purchase any deck you like as well as give them as gifts.

Many people are superstitious—OK, how about fussy?—about using only their own deck of cards to read with. That is an individual decision. Amy and I are happy to let others use our personal decks and touch our cards. We like to think it adds good energy and love to them. Your cards are special, so it is a good idea to keep your deck in a lovely pouch or cloth—this keeps your deck clean and protected.

Because many Tarot decks are sold bundled with books, like our sets, you can reliably find Tarot decks in bookstores—brick-and-mortar bookstores that you can actually walk into and online book stores such as BarnesandNoble.com, Amazon.com, and USGamesInc.com (U.S. Games Systems' Web site). In France, Tarot cards have traditionally been sold by tobacconists!

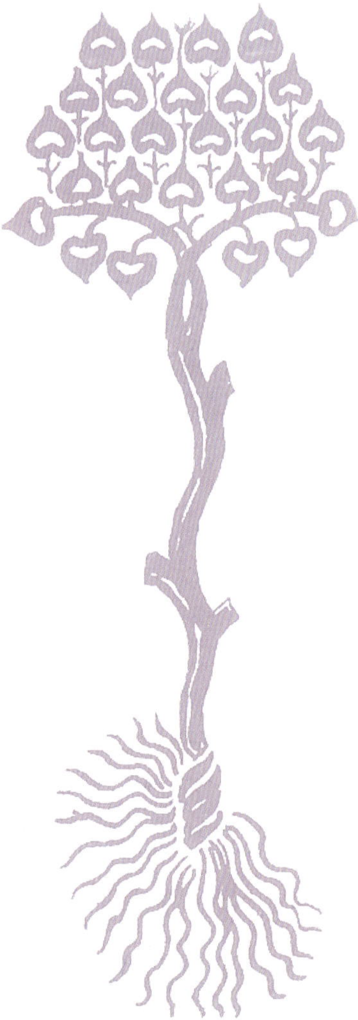

The problem with many of these book/Tarot deck kits is that the books they contain are often more confusing than they are helpful, especially to the new Tarot reader. This is why we have written *Tarot Secrets*.

What are the secrets for choosing which Tarot deck is right for you? Buying a deck online has its advantages, but it also has its drawbacks, mainly that you can't see all of the cards and you can't feel them. Not everyone uses a computer, but even if you do, going to your local bookstore or other store that sells Tarot cards is probably the best way to choose your deck. If you're lucky, someone who works there or who is also buying a deck can recommend a deck for you. It's not just the images that are important. The size of the deck has to fit your hand and the card stock has to be a comfortable thickness when you shuffle the cards.

Your local bookstore, especially if it is or was a New Age bookstore, may keep a loose-leaf binder whose pages display a few representative cards of the decks it offers for sale. U.S. Games Systems, one of the largest distributors of Tarot decks, supplies stores with a countertop display showing representative cards from many decks.

If your interest in Tarot comes from getting a reading in person from a friend or a professional reader, then you've seen at least one deck, maybe more. Most Tarot readers I know are delighted to show you their decks—they invariably have a collection of them—and usually are not shy about giving you their opinion on which deck might be good for you.

One great way to learn what a lot of your fellow Tarot readers think about the various decks is to go online and visit one or more of the great Tarot Web sites—there are a lot of them! The best of them have detailed reviews of decks that include a few sample card images.

There is a wonderful feeling of community surrounding the Tarot—there are even gatherings of Tarot readers for conventions on occasion. Whether you are choosing your first deck or your fiftieth, when you read Tarot cards you become yet another link in an unbroken chain of Tarot readers that stretches back in time. We are all standing on the shoulders of these courageous and wonderful people who helped keep the art of psychology and guidance counseling alive through the dark times of ignorance and superstition. But what exactly is a Tarot deck?

Tarot Secrets

We know your Tarot secret: You want to get on with doing your first Tarot reading! So we're now going to give you the minimum essential information you need to do so. We've placed the more in-depth information in essays at the back of this book for you to read at your leisure.

The biggest secret connected to the Tarot may be its origin. There are so many theories that we've put them in a separate chapter, "The Secret Origin of the Tarot," on page 154. Another secret is why Tarot cards are able to tell the future. We've put our explanation for that into a section called "The Secret of Why the Tarot Works," on page 155.

As we've said, *Tarot Secrets* is designed to enable you to read virtually any seventy-eight-card Tarot deck. The secret of why virtually all decks have that many cards is that Tarot decks may very well have started out as two separate decks: a twenty-two-card spiritually oriented deck whose purpose was religious instruction and divination, and a fifty-six-card deck used for gaming and gambling.

A seventy-eight-card Tarot deck uses twenty-two Major Arcana (meaning "greater secrets") cards (they each have a name, such as The Fool, The Magician, The High Priestess) and fifty-six Minor Arcana (meaning "lesser secrets") cards, ace through ten and then Princess /Page, Prince/Knight, Queen, and King, also known as the deck's "pip" cards.

The Major Arcana

The Twenty-two Spiritual Principles of Life

Forgive me for repeating myself, but it is the best way to help you remember this most important fundamental secret of the Tarot before you do your first reading. The Major Arcana is composed of the first twenty-two cards of the Tarot, starting with the card whose number is 0, The Fool, and going up to the card whose number is 21, The World. These cards represent the arcane or secret spiritual principles of life.

We all begin our journey as The Fool, newly born, innocent, and poised on the threshold of a great cycle of growth and experience; after learning the lessons symbolized by the other Major Arcana cards, we eventually arrive at The World, our graduation and the culmination of a major period of our life. Between these two cards are the twenty other major stages of spiritual growth and learning. Once we have gone through them all, we are ready to start again on a new major cycle of our soul's sacred quest for experience and self-knowledge. On page 156 you will find our essay "The Spiritual Journey Through the Major Arcana," which explains in detail this universal path to spiritual development.

In our opinion, one of the most important secrets of Tarot reading is that it enables us to incorporate our spiritual development into our daily activities and decisions. Using the power of the Tarot gives users a unique advantage over those not bold enough to explore all of their options for gathering and processing information for their spiritual development.

Few of us, however, are able to devote ourselves totally to our spiritual development as symbolized by the Major Arcana. It is rare to find people asking spiritual questions of the Tarot because most people don't realize that it can, indeed, answer them. Most people consult the Tarot for answers to their mundane, day-to-day questions and especially to help them to make important decisions. That is where the Minor Arcana come into play.

The Minor Arcana

Guidance for Daily Life

The cards of the Minor Arcana are not as concerned with spiritual realities as they are with our everyday, earthly reality as human beings. We are spiritual beings living in the world of matter and form, and so it is good to have a balance between the lofty goals of the spirit and our mundane (from *mundus*, meaning "of the world") needs. The Minor Arcana helps us to bring the spiritual wisdom of the Major Arcana down to earth so that we can use it for our benefit on all levels.

We believe that the cards of the Minor Arcana are the origin of the modern playing card deck, whose four suits—Clubs, Spades, Hearts, and Diamonds—are the descendents of the Tarot's traditional four suits—Wands, Swords, Cups, and Pentacles. You will notice that on her *Enchanted Tarot* deck and *Zerner-Farber Tarot Deck*, Amy used the shapes of the four playing card suits as a central organizing principle of the Minor Arcana suits—you can see a spade-shape background on the Swords cards, a diamond on the Pentacles cards, a club shape on the Wands cards, and, of course, a heart shape on the Cups cards.

Each suit also has four Court cards, comprised of a King, a Queen, a Prince or Knight, and a Page or, in the case of our decks, a Princess to establish gender equality. These "face cards" of the Tarot may represent the faces of people you are involved with or an aspect of your personality that you are dealing with at the moment.

I know you're champing at the bit to do your first reading, but, trust me, take a few minutes to familiarize yourself with the four suits and you'll have a much easier time understanding your first reading and every one that follows. Notice that we offer "Keywords" to help you get the feel of what each suit is all about. As you will soon see, we use the same keyword technique for all seventy-eight cards—keywords really help you to embed the various meanings in your consciousness.

WANDS

Wands (also known as Fire, Clubs, Roses, Scepters, or Rods) represent the active, transforming principle at work in human affairs. Wands indicate activity and busyness. They always warn against idleness and gossip. They denote movement and energy going in the right direction and advocate speed. The Wands indicate what action the "querent" or the "consultant," terms we use interchangeably to refer to the person asking the question, should take to create his or her destiny. They show the power of the querent to energize a situation.

KEYWORDS FOR WANDS

Business
Action
Judgment
Acumen
Alertness
Brevity
Speed
Order
Plans
Development

SWORDS

Swords (also known as Air, Spades, Blades, or Wings) symbolize aspects of the realm of ideas, the world of the mind and communication. By an inversion, the Sword card points to the mental force or thought to be used in order to get rid of discordant conditions. Swords are very valuable in uncovering any unknown faults or negative tendencies in the consultant's disposition.

KEYWORDS FOR SWORDS

Concepts
Conflict
Discussion
Opposition
Disharmony
Injustice
Inefficiency
Complexity
Doubt
Indecision

CUPS

Cups (also known as Water, Hearts, Chalices, or Shells) represent affection, love, intuition, and spiritual interests. They are closely connected with intuition, talent, emotions, and the general good. In ancient lore they represent the heart in humans. Hearts are the symbols of the basic principles of good and are given the sign of Cups. Viewed from this meaning, Cups may represent the home, family, and relationships.

KEYWORDS FOR CUPS

Love
Spirituality
Talent
Harmony
Empathy
Revelation
Sensitivity
Therapy
Partnership
Cooperation

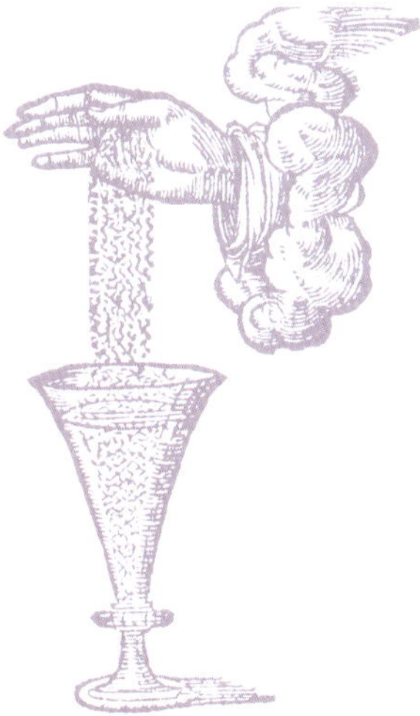

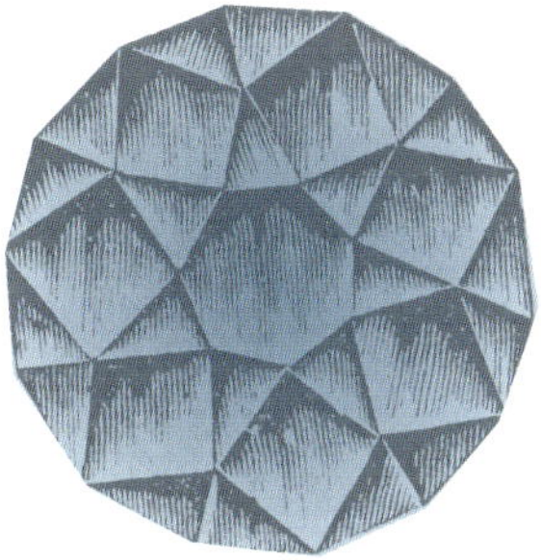

PENTACLES

Pentacles (also known as Earth, Coins, Gems, or Disks) are the life cards. They refer to the idea of a struggle in work and business, and manifestation. They are nearly always of financial influence. They symbolize inspiration coupled with production to create abundance, success, protection, affluence, and vitality. They also represent resources, development, and progress.

KEYWORDS FOR PENTACLES

Life
Abundance
Opportunity
Construction
Poise
Serenity
Values
Food
Jewelry
Clothing

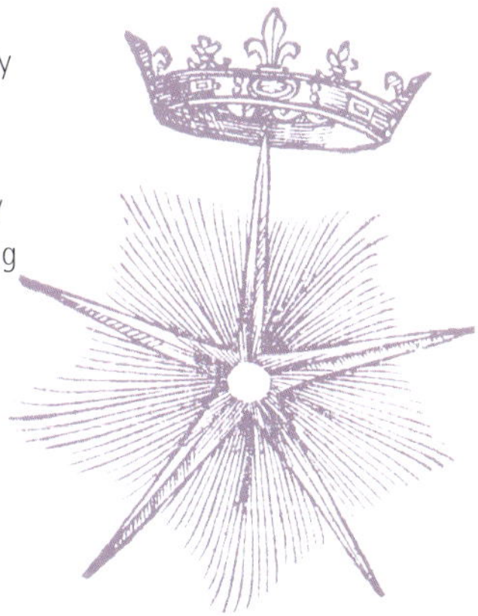

NUMERICAL SIGNIFICANCES ACROSS THE SUITS

While each card has an individual meaning, the cards belonging to the same number series show the same influence (positive or negative according to the suit). By studying the numerical significances, you will be able to further remember the meanings of the cards and classify them in your mind. Don't worry, you don't have to do this at all, but you can if you want to.

THE ACES

An ace signifies a beginning, an end, or a new chapter. One is the number of individuality.

THE TWOS

A two represents a premonition, a warning, a caution, a chance meeting, or a time-out.

THE THREES

Threes are mostly fortunate cards. They mean revelation, surprise, sympathy, purification, love, and celebration.

THE FOURS

Fours represent completion, realization of a project, or consultation. They mean the four corners of the city, house, church, bed, or table, as well as the four seasons.

THE FIVES

Fives represent the unknown influences and have a double meaning. They should always be read as a warning to the querent or consultant to deal with a negative quality and reestablish the positive.

THE SIXES

Sixes indicate success or failure. The positive side foretells artistic, literary, and harmonious instincts. The negative warns against excesses and addictions and forewarns of association with those of a bad influence.

THE SEVENS

Sevens show a change of interest, fortune, or residence. They also reveal happenings at a distance and events to take place in the future. They always warn the querent or consultant to exercise his or her utmost wisdom and to be an ardent seeker for truth and beauty.

THE EIGHTS

Eights represent the point where the consultant controls his or her own fate for failure or achievement, according to the energy given to the right or wrong side. Brooding over a discordant condition, a discourteous act, or discouragement should be strenuously guarded against.

THE NINES

Nines concern the highest wishes. They mean realization or disappointment. They are often indicative of psychic intuition. They counsel a change of project, wish, or pursuit, as there could be something even better in store for the consultant.

THE TENS

Tens represent the final aspect of the consultant's enterprise, home, or health. The ten foretells great benefits socially or with business, family, or wellness.

THE COURT CARDS

The Court cards represent influences and sometimes an actual person with the appearance and characteristics of that particular card.

Secrets for Shuffling, Cutting, and Asking Your Deck Questions

SHUFFLING

Shuffling the cards of the Tarot at the same moment you are concentrating on your question causes your question and the cards you select in answer to your question to be linked by the power of your intention and concentration. Your state of mind as you shuffle, cut, and draw your card(s) implies a future course of events in regard to the situation you are asking about. They are connected in a meaningful way because they are happening at the same time.

By shuffling and selecting one or more cards from your chosen deck as you calmly and sincerely ask for advice about your situation, we believe that you cause your Higher Self to guide you to select the proper card. Each Tarot card that you choose symbolizes and reflects a particular energy. Your Tarot reading will offer you a perspective on the situation you are inquiring about.

Before you start any Tarot session, you must remember that your state of mind must be positive, confident, and based on your desire to know the truth, whatever that may be. Always ask yourself or whomever you are reading for, "Do you really want to know the answer to these questions?" If you or the querent is open to receiving messages from the universe, the cards will capture the energies that are all around as they are shuffled and cut. We have included a section, "The Secret of Why the Tarot Works," on page 155, to explain this in more detail.

If you or the consultant or querent is in the midst of emotionally disturbing problems, it is necessary for you to take a few moments to calm and focus yourself before starting the session. Doing Tarot readings while you are emotionally unstable is a waste of time—you will never get clear information. You must first center yourself by taking three deep, long breaths in . . . and out slowly. Feel yourself calming down and becoming ready, willing, and able to hear what the universe has to tell you. If you or the querent cannot calm down, then don't do the reading.

Likewise, if you or the querent or consultant is under the influence of drugs or alcohol, then don't do the reading. If you don't heed these warnings, then don't be surprised if the answers you get in your Tarot readings are neither enjoyable nor accurate—don't insult the cards and make them angry with you! Also, do not ask the same question more than once or, again, you may find yourself getting some difficult cards—your deck's way of saying "Get serious!"

Only when you are in the right frame of mind should the cards be shuffled, a question meditated upon or spoken aloud, and then the individual card or cards chosen and arranged in a particular way (the spread). When you do a reading with a clear intention, your question aligns with the energies of the moment and an answer is given. The card or cards allow the energies of that answer to be offered to you. As the cards are interpreted, the answer is revealed.

Secrets of Asking Your Question

It's time! You are about to ask your first question of your Tarot cards. Tarot questions can be about any issue or problem.

There is an old saying among Tarot readers: If you know your question, you know your answer. This refers to the fact that the process of formulating your question, refining it so that you are asking what you really need to know in as precise a manner as possible, leads you closer to the answer to the question you have worked to formulate.

You'll need to ask the right question in the right way to get the appropriate solution or advice that you seek. In fact, if the answer you get doesn't seem to relate to your question, it is almost always a good idea to take a look back at how you phrased your question and try interpreting your answer in terms of how you've asked it.

A good Tarot reader must always keep in mind the question when interpreting the individual cards. At first, you may want to write your question down. Either way, we cannot overstate how important it is to phrase the question correctly. Make it as specific as possible.

Always say your question as you shuffle the cards, either to yourself or out loud. There is no right or wrong way to shuffle; just do it in a manner that feels comfortable to you. Here are some suggested ways in which you can phrase your one-card questions:

1. *Give me a message about _____ for my highest good and greatest joy.*
2. *Give me guidance and insight about _____?*
3. *What do I need to know about _____?*
4. *What is the meaning of _____?*
5. *What is the lesson or purpose of _____?*
6. *How am I perceived by _____?*
7. *What is going to be the future outcome of _____ if the present course is/is not changed?*
8. *How can I improve _____?*

How long you shuffle is also a personal choice. Shuffling seven times will ensure a good mixing of the cards. Amy and I stop and put the deck down on the table when we feel it is "cooked" and ready to be cut. I sometimes shuffle while visualizing in my mind's eye the High Priestess card and waiting for her to wink at me or otherwise let me know that I can stop shuffling.

Another method is to shuffle for as long as it takes to ask your question, but this works well only if you are a fast and thorough shuffler. If you are not, or if your question is a short one, then shuffle as you ask your question three times. If by doing this you realize that your question can be refined further, then certainly do so. The more precise your question, the easier it will be for your answer to be interpreted.

Over the years, Amy and I have found that if a card falls out of the deck when you are shuffling, you should not put it back! In almost all cases, we have found that the card is an important message about what you're asking about, so look up the meaning of the card that has fallen out of the deck and interpret it as an answer to your question. Then put it back in the deck and ask your question again. You may want to adjust your question based on the insight you might have gained from the card that jumped out of the deck. You can't fool your Tarot deck, though, so be assured that this only works when you are not trying to have a card jump out!

Once you've finished shuffling, put the deck down and cut the cards three times to the left with your left hand. In Tarot reading, cutting the deck symbolizes that you are cutting your attachment to the desire to obtain a particular answer to your question.

If you believe you will become upset if you get any answer other than the one you are seeking, then you are too attached to the answer you seek and should either calm yourself before proceeding or ask the question when you are not so obsessed. Even if you are not attached to a particular answer, there will be times when the answer you receive is not the one you hoped for. When that happens, ask question 8 (above) to find out how you can improve your chances of making things go the way you'd like them to.

Have faith in your ability to know the truth when you hear it and to act appropriately when you do. You can handle whatever life throws you, especially when you've been forewarned of coming challenges.

Have faith in your ability to know the truth when you hear it and to act appropriately when you do. You can handle whatever life throws you, especially when you've been forewarned of coming challenges.

With knowledge of the future comes the ability to guide the future, if you are willing to do the work. Amy and I like to take responsibility for what life brings our way because we believe that if our decisions and actions brought things to where they are now, then we have the power to make better decisions and work harder and smarter to bring things around to where we want them to go.

Pay attention when you are cutting the deck. Notice which stack of cards came from which part of the deck because once you have cut the deck into three stacks, you will put them back together so that the third stack, which was on the bottom of the deck, is now on the top of the deck, and the first stack, which was on the top of the deck, is now on the bottom.

Draw the required number of cards from the top of the deck. Don't turn them over until you have them all in place. When you turn them over, flip each card the same way using the same hand. It doesn't matter if you flip the cards top to bottom or side to side; what matters is that you are consistent. If a card appears to be upside down, *leave it that way! Tarot Secrets* offers different meanings for the same card depending on whether it is upright or reversed.

When you look up the meanings of your cards, read the interpretation according to its upright or reversed position. When a card is upright, its qualities are available, free, and active. When a card is reversed, its energy may be losing power or may be incomplete or undeveloped.

After you have turned over the card or cards and before you begin to read them, spend a moment looking at each card individually as well as the entire Tarot spread. This is an important practice for a Tarot reader of any skill level. We often think we know a card well, yet taking the time to look at the cards anew almost always reveals new correlations with recent events and influences.

The "Quick Read" that appears with each card—both upright and reversed—in *Tarot Secrets* is a short, to-the-point message from the card. We are all in a hurry and need a quick fix sometimes! The "Quick Read" simplifies the art of Tarot reading. Remember to always apply the message to the question; if you do so, your answers will make sense.

The "Secret," the last paragraph on the card's interpretation page, for both upright and reversed cards, gives you the core meaning of the card's fundamental nature and significance.

For an in-depth reading, refer to the entire explanation of each card, whether upright or reversed. This text gives more details that will clarify the significance of the card's relationship to your question.

After you've done enough one-card readings to have confidence in your knowledge of the cards, you can try to do the three-card Mind-Body-Spirit spread. Our advice when interpreting that and all the spreads is to read either *all* of the Keywords, *all* of the Quick Read answers, or *all* of the Secrets of each card in the layout, depending on what method you are using. We give example readings for each of the Master Spreads (see "The Twelve Master Spreads," page 109), showing you how to read with these fast and easy techniques that we have devised.

It is very important to allow your intuition to speak. If you do, then meanings, words, and messages will come to you, seemingly out of nowhere, messages that suddenly adapt perfectly to the layout to express correctly what the cards are trying to say.

Now it is time for you to formulate your question, say it while shuffling, cut the cards, choose one of them—it can be the top card or any one you choose, as long as you don't see which card it is before picking it—and look up the answer to your question in the following chapter.

Meanings and Secrets of the Seventy-eight Cards of the Tarot

THE CARDS OF THE MAJOR ARCANA

0 The Fool

KEYWORDS

• Trust • Innocence
• Playfulness • Leisure
• Adventure • Beginning

UPRIGHT

Quick Read: ***Have fun—you are truly blessed!***

• Don't be misled by a cursory reading of this card—the Fool card means that the world is your oyster now. All those prayers and wishes you have been harboring are about to pay off! The Fool signifies a total absence of self-consciousness and fear, indicating that this is the time to pull out all the stops. In other words, don't be afraid to just go for it!

• New enterprises aren't just likely now; they are positively encouraged, and you will be able to approach them with enthusiasm and self-confidence. Is there a much-cherished dream or goal that you haven't put into action because you are afraid of what you might be risking as a result? Put those worries aside and trust your deepest instincts. Count your blessings and take some time to play and enjoy yourself.

Secret: Fear is a four-letter word, especially now. Be adventurous. Taking chances and making leaps of faith that you might have been too timid to attempt in the past can lead to amazing rewards at this point in your life. The influence of an innocent and playful individual is favored.

REVERSED

Quick Read: ***Don't be foolish!***

• In the reversed position, the Fool can denote a time or an act of foolishness. You might find it hard to take yourself seriously now, or you may be deluded about something, most likely a relationship. Your naïveté can be a drawback at this point, especially if you trust your emotions instead of your common sense.

• While you may be anxious to pursue an adventurous and exciting lifestyle, you must first deal with important issues in your life. If you attempt to gloss over the serious aspects of a situation, you will find that your dreams are hollow and unlikely to come true and your plans remain unfulfilled. Make it a point to curb impulsiveness. Be more discerning, particularly when it comes to trusting new people in your life.

Secret: Stay away from gossip and silly, unprofitable behavior. It may seem harmless, but it could lead to trouble and misunderstandings. You could be deluded about yourself or someone else, thinking that you or the individual in question has wonderful qualities when that is not really the case. Alternatively, you may be led to make some foolish choices. It's time to be more serious.

1 The Magician

KEYWORDS

• Energy • Visualization
• Skill • Revelation
• Destiny • Manifestation

UPRIGHT

Quick Read: ***You've got the power!***

• It is time to take charge. The Magician represents the totality of the conscious mind and one's ability to focus and control it to make magic. This card means that there is more than just good luck working on your behalf; you are surrounded by a vibrant, charged atmosphere directed by powerful, universal forces. This card can also mean that a unique individual is about to come into your sphere and bring a strong element of enchantment into your life. This person has the ability to coax your creative talents out into the light.

• Take inventory of your skills and resources and prioritize them according to the goals you have at this time. Realize that you are a person of many gifts and talents, so don't overlook, belittle, or ignore them! Make a point each day to reaffirm your wishes and dreams. A talent you may not have realized you possess could emerge now.

Secret: Use your skill and intelligence to create a more brilliant reality for yourself. Truly, the sky is the limit. By channeling the positive energy of the universe and visualizing what you would like to see happen, you can manifest and enrich your future. Pretend that you are a magician asking the universe for what you want and expecting it to deliver right on time!

REVERSED

Quick Read: ***Not so fast!***

• Is there magic missing from your job, your relationship, or some other area of your life? A general lack of ambition and self-confidence could be a problem for you. It is possible that you have been struggling recently and as a result you have simply run out of steam. Alternatively, you might allow a person of questionable ability to exert too much influence on your life.

• The Magician reversed can indicate that you have given up, abdicating responsibilities and abandoning goals because you don't think you have the proficiency it takes to make them come true. There might be a lack of physical energy or a dearth of material resources on your part that instills a sense of apathy. While it can be hard to throw off this malaise, you need to take stock of your best traits and skills and then decide just how you can use them to improve your situation.

Secret: Remember that you are a co-creator of the universe! Whatever your circumstances are now, you can turn them around so long as you don't fear the power of your own abilities and creativity.

2 The High Priestess

KEYWORDS

- *Intuition* • *Receptivity*
- *Knowing* • *Philosophy*
- *Femininity* • *Meditation*

UPRIGHT

Quick Read: ***You know the answer.***

• When you feel inspired, you are inspiring to others—and the presence of this card indicates that you are awake and receptive to the dozens of miracles, both large and small, that happen in your life every day. The High Priestess invites you to tap into the deepest and most secret wisdom that you possess, trusting it above logic and common sense. You are now in a position where you need to pay attention to your inner voice because that is where your answers lie.

• This is a time to treasure all of life's small but amazing mysteries. You feel positively plugged in to everything from a child's laughter to the antics of a pet. You find beauty and mystery in your natural surroundings, and what may have seemed commonplace in the past is now infused with an almost otherworldly presence. You may be attracted to a person of mystery, utterly fascinated by the mystical connection the two of you appear to share.

Secret: Don't censor yourself. Some of the wisest insights are likely to come to you unbidden at this time. Forget the logical approach to solving a problem and rely on your psychic intuition instead.

REVERSED

Quick Read: ***Uncertainty and procrastination threaten.***

• This can be a hazy, unclear period; you seem to be receiving mixed messages from the universe. You are highly dependent on your intuitive faculties but may lack the sensitivity to decode them. Relying solely on prayer and your intuition can make you lazy, unwilling to face circumstances in a practical, commonsense way. Trying to find a balance between mystery and reality can be virtually impossible for you now.

• It is easy for you to become overly dependent on vague and illogical feelings, to the point where you become superstitious—fearful of making decisions on your own or unwilling to trust your own judgment. You might feel intimidated because a spouse or lover doesn't share your belief in metaphysical matters. While it helps to have the support of someone you love, a difference of opinion shouldn't cause you to feel unsure about your own beliefs.

Secret: The High Priestess reversed suggests that having too many secrets can work against you, especially if you are hiding the truth from yourself. Don't make life more complicated or weird than it is.

3 The Empress

KEYWORDS

• *Creativity* • *Beauty* • *Abundance* • *Harmony* • *Sensuousness* • *Birthing*

UPRIGHT

Quick Read: ***It's time for creativity.***

• This is one of the most fortunate cards among the Tarot's Higher Arcana. At this time you can be the beneficiary of great joy and happiness, especially through the auspices of the material world. Keep in mind that materialism itself is not bad—it all depends on how you use it. This is your time to be generous and even philanthropic because you have the means to do it.

• Your resourcefulness shows itself in a variety of ways at this time. If you are artistic, expect to give birth to a new project now. You also have the means to respond inventively to challenges, problems, or even out-and-out difficulties. Remember that your current situation could be one of your own creation. You will also demonstrate a talent for solving any of those challenges while still managing to nurture the interests of everyone you care about.

Secret: This is a wonderful time to align yourself with a creative person because this individual can have a positive effect on you. Give birth to a wonderful project that is beautiful, harmonious, and inspiring. Prosperity is also indicated.

REVERSED

Quick Read: ***Resources may pose problems.***

• Is there really such a thing as too much of a good thing? This card reversed suggests that it is likely. Even though this is sure to be a highly favorable time for you in many ways, you could easily allow material concerns to get in the way of family relationships, friendships, and other important personal aspects of your life. Certainly, wealth and good times are great, but you shouldn't let that divert you from more spiritual matters.

• Even if you do concentrate on personal concerns during this period, you could experience problems, especially where children or family are concerned. Moreover, financial restrictions may prevent you from making improvements to your surroundings or even your personal appearance, leaving you with a sense of frustration. The Empress reversed can also signify that your creative gifts are currently stifled, keeping you from expressing yourself in the way you would like.

Secret: Unresolved issues with important women in your past and present may reemerge now. You could suddenly discover that you have powerful and negative notions about prosperity and money that you didn't realize you held. Don't ignore your creative pursuits.

4 The Emperor

KEYWORDS

• Achievement • Benevolence • Power • Intractability • Leadership • Charisma

UPRIGHT

Quick Read: ***Climb the ladder to success.***

• This card is all about being tested and having the leadership qualities needed to stand up to such a test. This is your time to emerge as a leader; in fact, it is vital to your self-image. You will need to detach to project the proper image to others. There has probably never been a time when you were so absorbed by a desire to make goals come to fruition, and your work ethic is strong enough to make it happen. This is also a period when you could find yourself drawn to a relationship with an authority figure.

• Even if you are not in line for a promotion, you could suddenly find yourself thrust into a leadership role. This requires you to draw heavily upon management and leadership skills—whether or not you actually have them! Expect your mettle to be tested—emotionally, spiritually, and even physically. How you respond will pretty much determine your future.

Secret: Because you don't hide the fact that you want to achieve power, others might see you as cold, even ruthless. But people who support your climb to the top see only your charismatic and powerful personality.

REVERSED

Quick Read: ***Questions of power may pose problems.***

• The negative energy associated with the Emperor in reversed position is your inability to trust in your own talents. At this time you have a tremendous ambition to succeed, but you may be too timid to simply go for it. This could be due to a lack of experience on your part or a fear of failing. Your reaction to authority figures and the status quo is curious now. A person who meets this description could spell trouble for you at this time, especially if your communication styles are very different.

• Lethargy, as opposed to energy, is part of your problem now, because you just don't have the motivation, emotional or physical, to push you where you want to go. You might be driven to extremes. If you make a conscious or unconscious decision to abuse the power that you have, nothing favorable will result.

Secret: Someone who is an authority or father figure in your life could use his power over you in a controlling or dictatorial way. Detachment can hurt you. Unfortunately, you might be too unclear or intimidated to voice your own opinion.

5 The Hierophant

KEYWORDS

• Tradition • Authority
• Conformity • Belief
• Mentor • Reunion

UPRIGHT

Quick Read: ***Stay true to your beliefs.***

• The Hierophant card often suggests a desire for spiritual guidance. Perhaps you are currently facing a moral dilemma and as a result need to refer to a traditional religious or ethical code. There is a delicate balance demanded in your life whenever this influence is in place, because even though you may feel the desire to embrace new standards and ideas, you are also drawn to the intellectual or spiritual discipline of your past.

• It is time for you to step out on your own, though, eager to embrace your personal standards. In fact, you have the ability to be a moral influence on others at this time. You should not be fearful that you might come off sounding preachy, strict, and opinionated. By the same token, shy away from acting as if you have all the answers to life's important questions. Strike out on your own path, but don't expect others to follow.

Secret: Tradition is a wonderful thing, but it can also be an impediment to progress. Don't take a position simply because it accords with what you were taught during your formative years. Be true to what you believe now.

REVERSED

Quick Read: ***Tradition may work against you.***

• It is time for you to grow up! The Hierophant reversed can suggest a fear of moving forward because you are entrenched in the past, governed by outmoded mores and outdated values. Tradition is a fine thing, but only if you agree with the beliefs it espouses. Unfortunately, at this point you probably find it too overwhelming to go against the ethical status quo, whether you endorse it or not.

• It is possible that you choose to emulate someone you admire without realizing that your styles are very different. Also, avoid having an agenda that could box you into accepting certain rigid conditions that are no longer a part of your lifestyle. While it might be hard for you to embrace the differences you and a family member or close friend have, try to keep them from becoming a reason to tear the relationship apart.

Secret: Don't be a stick in the mud! No one should ever be so concerned with being right all the time that they refuse to embrace new ways of thinking. Work at being more flexible.

6 The Lovers

KEYWORDS

• Attraction • Pact • Relationship • Choice • Attunement • Consequences

UPRIGHT

Quick Read: ***Follow your bliss.***

• Whether or not you are currently in love, you will find yourself having to choose between two or more attractive allurements in the very near future. While this might seem to be a fortunate "problem," it could cause you a certain amount of trepidation. Ask yourself this question: Is the love I am seeking just a dream, or is it a reality? If you have eyes for someone and are unsure if your feelings will be reciprocated, this card indicates that the individual in question probably feels the same about you.

• The Lovers can also suggest that you will be faced with an important personal decision soon. It could reflect the choice between what you currently have and what you think you want. You could also find yourself confronted by contradictory sides of your own nature, not quite sure how to bring these opposing characteristics together in a harmonious blend of energies.

Secret: It may be a time to make an important decision, but if romance or passion is concerned, make sure it is really what and whom you want. This card can represent a love affair but doesn't necessarily predict a permanent commitment.

REVERSED

Quick Read: ***Examine your decisions carefully.***

• This card usually signifies romance, not partnership, but if you and a love interest have been moving in that direction lately, the Lovers reversed suggests that the relationship may somehow be lopsided. One of you has more power than the other; it is also possible that the two of you have different expectations about where the relationship is headed. Don't allow yourself to be so carried away by romantic feelings that you trade away your own interests and self-respect.

• There is also a chance that fear of making a wrong choice can keep you from making any choice at all, which is just as dangerous. An inability to make wise decisions can block your progress. While you shouldn't rush into making decisions, you should never avoid them, either, since both of these tactics preclude wise choices.

Secret: You are uncertain of whether or not to take a new relationship to the next level—mainly, establishing an intimate connection. Before you make that choice, be certain that you and your partner are ready for the emotional consequences that will ensue.

7 The Chariot

KEYWORDS

• *Determination* • *Control* • *Willpower* • *Goals* • *Preparation* • *Praise*

UPRIGHT

Quick Read: ***Listen to your head, not your heart.***

• There are times when you should let your emotions guide you—but this is not one of those times. Instead, take control and focus all your attention and energy on a specific enterprise. The crucial element at this point is the level of your commitment to an important goal.

• Don't allow yourself to be distracted or sidetracked. You have a race to win, so throw any sense of timidity to the winds.

• What is required for your ultimate success now is an adherence to the principle of hard work. If you are not accustomed to such concentrated effort, you had better get used to it. Harness all of your natural confidence and self-control in order to drive yourself forward. Be that take-charge type of individual that the universe wants you to be. Remember, the path to your goal is every bit as inspiring and satisfying as the destination itself.

Secret: A career or professional goal is likely to take precedence over personal relationships now. This may not be your usual style of prioritization, but it is what works best now. Take the reins and stay focused—you can win the race!

REVERSED

Quick Read: ***Beware of roadblocks and explore detours.***

• Even the best plans can be derailed if there are insurmountable odds blocking your progress. If that is the case, don't fool yourself by thinking that stubborn resistance alone will get you what you want. There is such a thing as being *too* focused on a plan, especially if all the indicators are showing that failure is imminent.

• Don't be too proud to admit that you might have taken a wrong turn or two; once you have realized that fact, it is up to you to make a definite course correction. Don't become defensive—if someone who matters to you and whose judgment you trust gives you advice on the matter, listen to what that individual has to say. If the problem is that you don't really know what you want, you need to get things straight in your mind. Simply wanting to be successful isn't enough. There needs to be a guiding sense of purpose or this journey will be like attempting to drive a vehicle without being able to steer it.

Secret: When the Chariot is reversed, it is not uncommon to experience problems concerning transportation or travel arrangements. You may have to give up a plan, cancel a trip you were anticipating, or rethink or revise a daily commute.

8 Strength

KEYWORDS

• *Brave heart* • *Devotion* • *Instinct* • *Loyalty* • *Allegiance* • *Endurance*

UPRIGHT

Quick Read: ***You are stronger than you think.***

• The key to being strong and heroic isn't that you are braver than the average human being but that you choose to go on in service to a greater cause despite your fear. There are many levels of strengths—emotional, intellectual, physical, spiritual—and there is no telling which of these will be most useful to you at this time.

• This card can represent a constant attempt to balance the spiritual and carnal elements in your nature. Rather than keeping them in harmony, the result could be a virtual seesawing from one extreme to the other. Even in the face of this conflict, you can find a way to integrate these "virtues"—for they are permanent and necessary aspects of our humanity. One of the things you may need to learn is how to be more loving and accepting of another person's weaknesses. When you get to that point, you will be equally forgiving of your own.

Secret: At this time, it is possible to accomplish with love what you can't do with force. Courage and perseverance are key; a brave heart can endure even where there is great fear. Be loyal and devote yourself to your higher ideals while paying attention to your instincts.

REVERSED

Quick Read: ***Remember, you're only human.***

• There are times when, despite your best efforts and intentions, you simply cannot rise to the level of selflessness, sacrifice, or strength that may be required. This card in reverse suggests that you need to beware of displaying cowardice or even reckless bravery in the face of challenging circumstances because it could prove to be your undoing.

• Strength reversed can mean that you are presently in the position to dominate others or have allowed yourself to be dominated by someone. You must avoid arrogance at all costs—someone else's or your own. Remember that a bullying or overly aggressive attitude is nothing more than weakness and self-doubt masquerading as strength. Do not give your power away in a misguided attempt to forge a closer relationship with someone you love; it will only end up cheating both of you.

Secret: Never lose sight of the fact that kindness is not weakness. You can be gentle without letting down your guard or being manipulated by others. True strength comes when you know who you truly are and what values you personify.

9 The Hermit

KEYWORDS

- *Introspection* • *Mysticism*
- *Eccentricity* • *Wisdom*
- *Counsel* • *Teacher*

UPRIGHT

Quick Read: ***Mastery is the path to wisdom.***

• This card suggests someone who is very good at he or she does. Of course, a hermit is a cautious loner or eccentric, too. Though this card may or may not describe you, it may represent a period in your life when you need to retreat to devote yourself to finding peace and calm in your mind and heart. If you are a highly sociable type who generally enjoys being surrounded by people and events, this could prove to be a challenging stretch, but it is a path you need to travel all the same.

• A current dilemma or concern requires total attention and dedication. It could reflect a new career path that forces you to focus more narrowly on professional instead of personal endeavors. This is the time to sequester yourself in order to learn and grow, so don't resist it. Study, read, and be contemplative to absorb the wisdom and express the mastery that will take you to the next level.

Secret: A deep sensation of alienation or isolation could surround you or someone you love now. There is also the chance that the influence of an older, wiser individual could be felt at this time—someone who can act in the role of mentor.

REVERSED

Quick Read: ***Don't hide your abilities.***

• When the Hermit is reversed, it often means that you should be careful because you will be unable to read your current situation accurately. You could misjudge your own or someone else's abilities or mistake their intentions. There is also a chance that a lack of introspection could block your progress. You may think that because you have learned a lot at this point, that in itself is enough. The real proof of just how far you have come in your journey, however, is the wisdom you have accumulated along the way.

• This is a time when you need to look deep inside yourself for answers because you will not find them anywhere else. This is a good time to devote yourself to silence and meditation. Avoid distractions whenever possible. Now, more than at any other time in your life, you must walk your own path.

Secret: A lack of social interaction or involvements can leave you feeling disconnected from those in your circle. Friends might feel neglected by you, and you might experience occasional bouts of depression or loneliness.

10 The Wheel of Fortune

KEYWORDS

- Cycles • Surprise
- Timing • Karma
- Fortune • Luck

UPRIGHT

Quick Read: ***Take a chance.***

• Rejoice—the good times are here! You shouldn't regard this as purely coincidental, though. Whether or not you realize it, you have been preparing for this cycle of fortunate circumstances for a long while. Good luck is actually a merger of skill, preparation, and opportunity, and that is where you find yourself at this point in time.

• Your intuition is a finely tuned instrument now; it will not lead you astray. Opportunities that suddenly appear before you may bring the success and rewards you have been dreaming of. There is a turn for the better, so don't be afraid to take a chance—luck is with you.

Secret: You are currently reaping the benefits of good deeds and positive actions from your past—both in this lifetime and in others. People you have helped will be anxious to help you in return. Some of these actions may be so subtle that you hardly notice them, yet they will bring a positive, lucky vibe into your life.

REVERSED

Quick Read: ***Don't gamble.***

• There is no such thing as a free lunch—even on the cosmic level! At this point in time you could find yourself saddled with a karmic debt that requires a certain amount of personal sacrifice on your part. You might not understand just how this works or to whom you owe an act of kindness, but you will soon learn.

• You are entering a new cycle, and at the onset this could seem to be an unlucky time. Even though you want good luck, a part of your nature simply cannot believe that it is your due. Remember, the flip side of good luck is bad luck. Once you have paid off this karmic obligation, you will be clear of obstacles once again, to begin a new positive cycle.

Secret: Although you have tremendous opportunities ahead of you, things seem to be stalled and stagnant now and in the near future. Because of this, it can be hard to motivate yourself. Also, fear of failure is your worst enemy. This period of stalemate will pass and you will be better off for having experienced it.

11 Justice

KEYWORDS

- Truth
- Structure
- Paperwork
- Adjustment
- Morality
- Legal matters

UPRIGHT

Quick Read: ***You reap what you sow.***

- Justice is a card that denotes a need for balance and emotional equilibrium in your life. Truth is the greatest gift you can give yourself at this time, because if you can be truthful to yourself you can also be truthful to others, and your life will be improved as a result. Justice will prevail if you have earned it through truth and your actions. You can expect your family life to be exceedingly peaceful and rewarding now. Children will be respectful, and a mate and friends will give you the attentiveness and hold you in the esteem you have earned.
- This is an excellent time to put things in writing—a will, an agreement, such as a prenuptial agreement, or another important legal document. Knowledge of and adherence to the law is vital now, because any slipups could be dangerous and damaging.

Secret: Lawyers and the law could have a place in your life for good or ill. Because of this, it is a good idea to keep clear of scandal or any type of dishonesty. Avoid volunteering too much information. Be prepared. Stay balanced and centered. Justice will be served.

REVERSED

Quick Read: ***All bills must be paid.***

- Relationship problems you have now are likely to be accentuated by lies and an attitude of restlessness on the part of you or your mate. You might think that playing hardball means giving back any unkindness you're getting from others, but that is the worst thing you can do. Forgiveness may be hard for you now, but even if you can't manage it, do your best to be tactful and discreet.
- If your concerns are not relationship oriented, they may have to do with legal or professional matters that do not go your way. Agreements may not be upheld in your favor, or an individual or company you have cause to trust may prove to be dishonest. You should be wary of someone who tries to maneuver you into a legal agreement or commitment since this individual is unlikely to be on the up-and-up. Just because you want to feel settled, there is nothing to be gained from rushing into an agreement, personal or financial, that seems questionable. The phrase *lingering doubts* rings true—remember it.

Secret: If you have a financial arrangement with a family member or former spouse, you could find yourself on the wrong end of legal demands. Don't try to get out of such obligations now. Be aware of imbalances or putting your faith in someone or something that does not deserve it.

12 The Hanged Man

KEYWORDS

• Suspension • Waiting • Vulnerability • Transition • Delays • Hang-ups

UPRIGHT

Quick Read: ***Change your perspective.***

• This card denotes a period when circumstances keep you from doing what you would ordinarily do. You cannot rush to make decisions about big or small matters because on some level you accept the fact that the best attitude to adopt now is one of introspection.

• A feeling of pause surrounds you, acting as a buffer against the urgency of achievement. Subconsciously, you are aware that this is a waiting period when you need to resist a quick-fix attitude, but you must not allow boredom or inertia to be an obstacle to your will to act. Being patient—not emotionally paralyzed—should be your goal. Quietly facing facts and being ready to deal with whatever new set of circumstances the universe chooses to toss your way are the answer to this malaise.

Secret: Don't waste time feeling sorry for yourself. What you want will come—in time. Some level of anxiousness or restlessness is to be expected, but being able to exhibit trust in the status quo is a definite plus! Take time to process and slowly add more stimulation to your routine.

REVERSED

Quick Read: ***Do not be egotistical.***

• The Hanged Man reversed suggests that you not only feel stymied at this time; you may feel powerless as well. Not being able to trust your own judgment might be a problem. More than likely, you might lash out, even if you feel your self-esteem plummet, as you feel unworthy of the people and the opportunities surrounding you.

• Stop! While you may be in a slump of some sort, that is not to say that you are completely off your game. The best way to deal with the cosmic influences at play in your life right now is to accept delays and hang in there for a while. A sacrifice or two may be necessary along the way, but don't make it at the expense of your future or reputation. Your talents, abilities, and intelligence are intact—and even if they don't seem to be doing you a great deal of good now, they'll be ready to help you move forward again when the time is right.

Secret: Be cautious, but don't be fearful. If delays produce complex circumstances that are beyond your control, try looking at them from a whole new perspective. If you are hung up on negativity, it is likely you will stay in a rut and miss the opportunities the universe has in store for you.

13 Death

KEYWORDS

• Transformation • Endings • Relinquishing • Awareness • Renewal • Surrender

UPRIGHT

Quick Read: ***Prepare for a big change.***

• This card shouldn't be read literally. It is not about physical death but rather reflects the transitions and periods of adjustment that occur naturally in life when we are confronted by the end of something. While it might be hard to let go of things, events, and relationships, keep in mind that in order for new changes, new interests, and new growth to come your way, you must first be willing to give up your hold on the past. Instead, concentrate your thoughts and energy on the present and the future. Personal transformation is the key to using this current energy to your best advantage.

• The Death card can also relate to the end of a job or other opportunity. Despite the trepidation you might be feeling, you are currently surrounded by universal energy that supports change and personal transformation on a profound level.

Secret: It is time to come to terms with a new reality. That doesn't mean that old habits or beliefs were wrong—they have simply worn out their welcome. Once you realize that you can find fulfillment in your new life, you will be less likely to stay with the status quo and more curious about what is coming your way.

REVERSED

Quick Read: ***Resistance is futile.***

• There is a saying that teaches us to "let go and let God." When this card is in the reversed position, it signals that your obstinacy is likely to block new progress in your life because you refuse to adhere to this wise maxim. We never "get over" the pain of loss; we only learn how to go on living with this new chapter in our life.

• To fear the ending of things is to fear life. You must transform yourself in order to start over once again. Endings set the stage for new beginnings, but until you are ready to accept that, your life may be unsatisfactorily impacted by a series of mistakes, misjudgments, and other problems. For example, if you try to hold on to a relationship that is no longer working, you will be disappointed by the outcome no matter how many personal sacrifices you make to facilitate it.

Secret: Paramount to your refusal to accept change now is a fear that it will cause you some sort of unbearable pain. That may not be the case, but even if it is, it is necessary. Destroy old ways of doing things and you will be rewarded as a new path opens up before you.

14 Temperance

KEYWORDS

• *Patience* • *Synthesis* • *Forgiveness* • *Healing* • *Moderation* • *Blending*

UPRIGHT

Quick Read: ***Easy does it.***

• Say good-bye to extremes of all sorts. This card denotes the importance of moderation in all circumstances. Now is not the time to be impetuous in any area of your life. A slow, measured, and well-considered approach is what you need in order to be successful at this point in time.

• This doesn't mean you should be afraid to experiment—but keep the importance of prioritization constantly before you. An incident or personal matter is likely to require more restraint than you are accustomed to displaying. Even if this situation is more complex than you originally perceived it to be, don't rush your response, because it could be detrimental. Instead, channel your energy in a way that promotes a slow and steady approach, such as making comprehensive lists of what you want and what you don't want—and the steps you need to take in order to ensure both.

Secret: Blending time, endurance, and your resources in a tolerant way is crucial to your situation. No matter how much urgency you may feel, it is necessary to allow events to evolve in their own time. Impatience is your worst enemy now. Nothing can be gained by rushing or forcing.

REVERSED

Quick Read: ***Don't be too stubborn.***

• The significance of Temperance reversed can be one of two things—either restlessness or almost total inertia. You want to act but are frustrated by your inability to make things happen quickly on your own. Naturally, there is a big difference between true temperance and the sort of laziness or apathy that comes from being complacent.

• You can easily fall victim to the advice or counsel of others now, and even if what is said is meant to be helpful, you are not doing yourself a favor if you allow yourself to be influenced in this way. By the same token, you must not ask too much of yourself. It is not possible to will things to happen at this time, so tread the path between acceptance and initiative with great skill.

Secret: Knowing exactly what you want is the key to getting it, even when you have to wait for events to coalesce on their own. If you are exceptionally inflexible or too pragmatic about what you want, you are likely to miss out on some wonderful opportunities.

15 The Devil

KEYWORDS

• *Trickery* • *Gratification* • *Lust* • *Negativity* • *Challenges* • *Addiction*

UPRIGHT

Quick Read: ***Play to win, but play carefully.***

• It is time to change your quest from one of material gain to one in which spiritual concerns take precedence. The Devil card suggests that even though worldly things have the power to seduce you, you should remember that you have the willpower to overcome that temptation. There are forces at work seeking to deceive, and no matter how cleverly you play the game, there can be lies, trickery, and subterfuge in your midst. Metaphorically speaking, you need to keep your cards close to the vest now.

• Under this influence, your challenge is to become more spiritually aware, as there may be negative influences at work. This card represents excesses, and because of this it may be hard for you or someone you care about to curb an addiction such as drinking, drugs, or an unwise romantic relationship. You have the strength to move beyond these emotional or physical limitations. Can you look past temporary gratification in order to ensure your progress?

Secret: There is the possibility that someone who has an important place in your life is lying to you or manipulating you. Trickery is definitely in the works, too, so watch your step. You may be held prisoner by your own demons. Play the game when it comes to business, but remember that it is only a game.

REVERSED

Quick Read: ***Wear a mask.***

• There is a popular maxim that instructs, "Keep your friends close and your enemies closer." That is a good way to describe your attitude now. This is a time when you need to act with subtlety in everything you do. Unfortunately, it can be difficult, if not impossible, for you to mask your true intentions. Certain people you are currently dealing with are likely to have an agenda all their own, though, and it doesn't favor you! It is best for you to resist beginning a relationship at this time, since it is impossible to know whom you can trust.

• If a current relationship has problems, it is likely that one of you is lying to the other or being deceitful in some other way. Whether or not you are the offending party, you will probably be unable to effect a satisfactory reconciliation, though there is a great deal at stake.

Secret: Sex without love is meaningless, so don't expect a love affair that is devoid of true affection and caring to work. In truth, you will soon come to rue such an arrangement. Don't take big risks in business, either. You might not win this time.

16 The Tower

KEYWORDS

• Crisis • Liberation
• Flux • Upheaval
• Freedom • Release

UPRIGHT

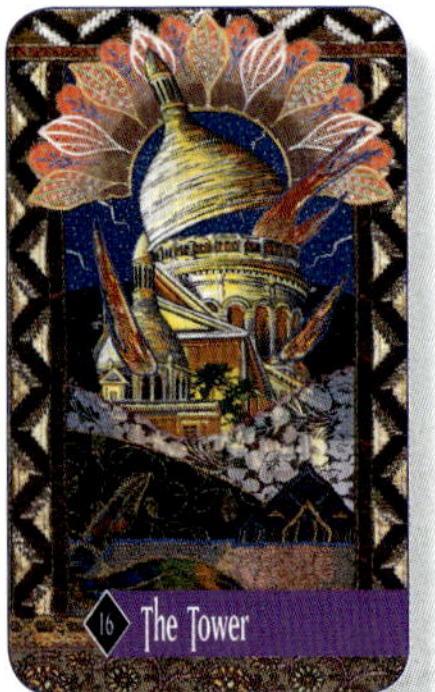

Quick Read: ***Expect the unexpected.***

• Big changes are headed your way—and soon! You will experience a dramatic shift in your life, like a hurricane or other storm that shakes things up. Beliefs, events, even people you have put your trust in for a very long time may be preempted suddenly in some way. This might appear to be a frightening scenario, but it can actually prove to be a helpful turn of events if you prepare wisely and weather the storm.

• Wherever and whenever there is havoc or risk, there is the chance to achieve wonderful things, but only after you survive the time of upheaval. Occasionally this card can be a warning, but usually only for those who are not willing to bring newness into their lives, prepare for the unexpected, or make necessary adjustments before, during, or after a big change.

Secret: You might find yourself drawn to an eccentric individual or unstable situation at this time due to an unexpected turn of events. Whether the relationship is romantic, professional, or strictly friendly, you can use it as a chance to grow spiritually by facing your limitations.

REVERSED

Quick Read: ***Beware of panic mode.***

• In times of crisis, people often act out of fear or desperation rather than from a place of common sense. You might think you know how you will respond to a sudden crisis in your life, but most likely that is not the case. While you may have the opportunity to reinvent yourself or take your life in a different direction because of a change in circumstances, you may be thrown off balance. Like a deer caught in the headlights, you must not hesitate, or it could be damaging to your cause.

• If there are problems in a romantic relationship, the situation could become tumultuous now, to the point where you either end the romance prematurely or stay in it out of fear and desperation. While you should not be afraid of change, you shouldn't embrace it as a solution to chaos. Do not destroy what is working for you.

Secret: The Tower reversed could represent a sudden and much-needed break from old rules, structures, or habits that no longer serve a useful purpose in your life. This crisis could bring a sense of liberation that could propel you forward to do what needs to be done, and make a fresh start.

17 The Star

KEYWORDS

• *Illumination* • *Peace*
• *Rejuvenation* • *Art*
• *Optimism* • *Purification*

UPRIGHT

Quick Read: ***Serendipity awaits.***

• The appearance of this card reminds you that at the present time you are surrounded by many wonderful possibilities—joy, hope, emotional healing, perhaps even fame! If you are looking for love, you could be on the brink of falling for the most enchanting and wonderful person you have ever known. It is time for you to step up as the star of your own show. Surrounding yourself with beauty—both material and spiritual—will help you to illuminate the beauty in yourself.

• If you have recently undergone a stressful or demanding period, this is your chance to experience a new cycle of peace and healing. Treat yourself to a vacation, a spa day, or a new hobby in order to reestablish the important connection with your body. This may also serve to enhance your personal vitality and give you a new lease on life.

Secret: Avoid negativity at all costs. Open up to inspiration. You need to use this time to nurture good feelings. If you daydream about what you want and balance it with practical actions, then your dream will come true.

REVERSED

Quick Read: ***Give up on what is not working.***

• The Star reversed suggests that you may be feeling uncharacteristically pessimistic. It is possible that a lover or cherished friend has let you down recently, causing you to question your talent for attracting love and affection. If you are a naturally creative person, you might experience a stagnant period when you worry that the channels of artistic expression have been blocked, at least temporarily.

• Spiritually, the Star in the reversed position indicates that you could be feeling uninspired. Even if you have a plan of action that will direct you, your heart probably isn't in it right now, making you feel as if you are just going through the motions. There is a small chance that you are feeling physically unwell, no doubt brought on by emotional stresses and strains. Because you don't trust your judgment, it can be very hard for you to make choices at this time. It is important for you to remember that giving up on your dream will only make you more apathetic and unsure.

Secret: Even if a promising relationship beckons, you probably won't pursue it because you feel disillusioned. Cynicism and hopelessness have set in, making it hard for you to trust that renewed optimism and true love really exist.

18 The Moon

KEYWORDS

- Night journey • Dreams
- Serendipity • Illusions
- Confusion • Warning

UPRIGHT

Quick Read: ***Journey through the unknown.***

- Because your path might seem murky and ill defined at this time, you may need to navigate via instinct rather than intellect or common sense. It is a time to focus on your inner world. The Moon card denotes an influence that can be hard to fathom. You may be somewhat disoriented, even afraid of what lies ahead. You might feel overly emotional. The answer to handling this confusing time is to get in touch with your dreams. Record them on a regular basis. By analyzing your sleeping thoughts, you can find answers to the questions that bedevil you.
- While it might be hard for you to separate illusion from reality now, it is important to steer clear of dangers, both physical and spiritual. It is tough to go on without a clear picture of your path, but the Moon's rays through the clouds will help show you the way.

Secret: Under this influence your house isn't just your castle; it is your sanctuary. At this time you may be inspired to redecorate your home or make it more beautiful in some way. Realize that delays and moodiness can hinder you. Listen to your intuitive hunches.

REVERSED

Quick Read: ***All expectations are unreasonable.***

- This is not an easy time. What was once mere confusion could turn into chaos. While the Moon reversed does not change it's meaning to a great degree, it can indicate that you are slower than usual at coming to grips with your feelings and interpreting your innermost desires. Even if you are normally self-aware, you could discover during this period that intuition has deserted you, making it hard to decipher your feelings when there is so little clarity.
- Do not be surprised if you are moody and disagreeable now. It is very hard to keep an even, upbeat temperament when you are feeling blue. Regarding plans for the future, it is likely that you are just as apprehensive—highly motivated one minute and uncaring the next. Finding your way through this bewilderment is virtually impossible, but if you can allow yourself to withstand this sense of vulnerability, things will improve over time.

Secret: A difficult relationship may cause you some consternation at this time. You may have been led astray, and you also have had a tendency to depend too much on relationships as a means of solving your problems. You may feel uneasy and insecure, without a firm foundation.

19 The Sun

KEYWORDS

• *Radiance* • *Validation*
• *Support* • *Empowerment*
• *Individuality*
• *Happiness*

UPRIGHT

Quick Read: *Happy days are here again.*

• The Sun is one of the most positive cards in the Tarot deck. Its influence radiates love, success, happiness, and creative energy. You are about to enter a new phase of your life when both your professional and private fortunes are enhanced in many ways. This is a time to celebrate your past accomplishments and prepare for future ones. Don't be tempted to hide your light under a bushel. Instead, proclaim to the world who you are and where you are going.

• There is so much positive energy swirling about you now that you feel as if the universe has singled you out for blessings. Because your creative gifts are at their zenith, this is the time to unfurl a new project, something that truly reflects your talents and heart. Gifts and acclaim come to you with ease.

Secret: Happiness and a love of life are in the air. Your natural charm and charisma have a strong effect on others now. There could be a wonderful new relationship on the horizon. Home and family situations are sunny and bright. Let your light shine.

REVERSED

Quick Read: *Don't be too sure of yourself.*

• Because this is such a fortunate card, the Sun reversed doesn't present too much of a challenge. It is possible that you are in a flourishing phase but not quite ready to blossom. You may still have some kinks to work out where your goals are concerned. Perhaps you feel that you are still in the student phase of your life. Since the Sun reflects the self, the ego, the Sun card reversed often means that you haven't yet grown into the image you wish to project to others.

• You could also experience problems because of an inflated ego. Because you are receiving so much attention and validation at this time, it is easy for you to let it all go to your head. Also, since you are feeling so happy now, it can be hard for you to be sensitive to the needs of others. You may even have to remind yourself to pay more attention to the people in your life that you love the most.

Secret: It may be time to question whether or not you have developed the sense of independence you need in order to be happy and successful. It is likely that a parent or other authority figure is pressuring you unfairly, and you may feel it as a blow to your ego.

20 Judgment

KEYWORDS

- *Reckoning* • *Atonement*
- *Urgency* • *Realization*
- *Decision* • *Evolution*

UPRIGHT

Quick Read: ***You are about to be tested.***

• The Judgment card tells you it is time to face your future without fear. You can sense that the time to settle accounts is coming—a major change that has the power to shake up your world. Now is the time when you are compelled to evaluate your past actions. Look at how your attitude and beliefs have changed during your life. Who are you now? Are you achieving your goals? If you don't like what you see, decide what you want and what you must do in order to improve things.

• Are you ready to move on to the next phase of your life? It is possible that you are not. You are about to gain insight by being tested. If a relationship is in flux, you could be in the position of deciding what needs to change in order to move it forward. Take responsibility for past mistakes and revitalize your union through kindness, love, and common sense.

Secret: Be decisive and don't hesitate. An important part of your life that has lain dormant is about to rise to the surface. Reconciliation is in the air. You are being called to account for your past actions—it's time.

REVERSED

Quick Read: ***Avoid being thin-skinned and defensive.***

• The Judgment card in the reversed position suggests that you may have to undergo a harsh assessment of your character from others. Whether or not their criticism is in any way warranted, you might feel the proverbial wind go out of your sails. You could find yourself having to deal with criticism from a former spouse or lover, and as a result you might be uncomfortable or unhappy for a while.

• It is important to court forgiveness now—forgive others for the real (or imagined) harm they have done to you. You should also forgive yourself for falling short of your own expectations. If you are hung up on a situation in your life that you don't know how to change, it can be hard to get beyond it at this time. You want things to change, but you don't really know how to bring that change about. What you need at this time is total honesty about who you are and what you want. Don't lie to yourself or make excuses—it will only deter you from success.

Secret: Your inner critic can render the strongest judgment of all at this time. You feel you were indecisive and didn't rise to a challenge correctly. Berating yourself for mistakes you might have made can undercut your self-esteem.

21 The World

KEYWORDS

Culmination • Awareness • Graduation • Expansion • Announcement • Discovery

UPRIGHT

Quick Read: ***Graduation day has arrived.***

• The world is yours! After a period of intense study, hard work, and self-evaluation, you have finally arrived at the very pinnacle of success. This is the time you have been waiting for, so act now and act boldly. A long cycle has ended and a new one is about to begin. This is one of the most important and meaningful times in your life, and it is up to you to make your dreams come true. It is time to throw off old habits and worn-out ways of thinking.

• *New and improved* should be the watchword for your future endeavors. Don't make the mistake of thinking that everything will be easy—you will have to work very hard to put your goals into action, but the rewards, both material and spiritual, are certain to be great!

Secret: Take a look at your life in the context of the long view, not short-range goals. Don't be afraid to leave your own little corner of the world, literally and figuratively. You can dance for joy! International connections or travel may be indicated.

REVERSED

Quick Read: ***You're not there yet.***

• You have learned a great deal, but believe it or not, you might still have a long way to go. This card in the reversed position tends to emphasize that you may not have fully absorbed the knowledge that you have been exposed to. In the case of a career or important personal relationship, you might be unsure if you have settled on the right path for you. Don't simply assume that because you feel good about the way things are going you have nothing more to learn. The attainment of wisdom is an ongoing process.

• Make certain that the world you are about to enter allows the freedom of choice you are looking for and deserve. It might be tempting to frame your aspirations according to what a mate, parent, or mentor expects of you. This is your life, so it is up to you to handle it in a way that best makes you feel whole. It may take a while, but you will learn how to put your learning experiences into perspective.

Secret: It will be a trying time, but a necessary one for inner growth. Knowledge and maturity don't always go hand in hand. You have accumulated much knowledge during your recent sojourn, but you must develop the maturity to use it in the most beneficial way possible.

WANDS

(also known as Fire, Clubs, Scepters, Rods, or Roses)

Ace of Wands

KEYWORDS

- *Initiation* • *Breakthrough*
- *Power* • *Potential*
- *Self-confidence*
- *Originality*

UPRIGHT

Quick Read: ***First impressions say it all.***

• Get ready to take on the world! This is a time when passion and energy take over your life. You are in a position of strength, indicating that if you are going up against someone, you are sure to have the upper hand. You are poised to make the first move, so focus your energy and break through each and every barrier. Others will marvel at your passion, creativity, and enterprising spirit. You can be a strong motivational force to others now. Not only are you able to impress, but you also can inspire them.

• Where personal relationships are concerned—familial, romantic, or friendly—there is a real chance for growth and improvement. At this time you feel positive, self-confident, and assertive, which automatically makes you a better friend, lover, or mate. If you choose to make new friends or improve a current relationship, you are certain to be richly rewarded. Don't second-guess yourself—go for it.

Secret: In an effort to reveal your abilities, you will be involved in the initiation of a bold new project. There will be a breakthrough, and a testing of your nerve as well as your talent. When you take action, be determined and be direct.

REVERSED

Quick Read: ***Look before you leap.***

• There is little question that you are eager to start work on a new endeavor, but being too impulsive, aggressive, or even timid could turn the endeavor into an errand of folly. Alternatively, you may have hesitated at the precise moment when you should have acted boldly to begin your task, and lost out on your great chance as a result. A lack of trust, honesty, or energy could derail your ambition for a current project. You should also beware of being so involved in your work that you experience emotional burnout.

• The Ace of Wands reversed could indicate that there is a lack of intimacy in a relationship, or that one of you may be more in love than the other. If there is too little real affection and understanding between the two of you, you might as well give up on it before you allow yourself to get too emotionally involved.

Secret: You want to have the energy and enthusiasm to initiate something new, but fear of the unfamiliar could be blocking your progress. Either your energies are too scattered or you might need to refocus on a more attainable goal.

Two of Wands

KEYWORDS

• Planning • Courage • Contemplation • Perspective • Assessment • Outlook

UPRIGHT

Quick Read: ***Make a plan.***

• You have come to a crossroads, and although you currently find yourself in a position of power, there are important choices you need to make. This is a time to look back over where you have come from and toward the place you wish to go, both personally and professionally. To make this happen, you need to carefully assess your situation and plan for the future without being overly anxious about it.

• Keep telling yourself that so long as you take everything important pertaining to this matter into account, you will arrive at a successful conclusion. Your challenge is to realize that you aren't in this alone—a partner, spouse, or business associate is likely to be involved in the enterprise. Because the two of you are so closely bound, either by affection or by creative inspiration, a joint endeavor has the potential to be highly successful.

Secret: Don't ignore the details of your new plans—the details are just as valuable as the bolder strokes. Keeping these two aspects of a goal in balance will ensure not only success but happiness as well. Make a list.

REVERSED

Quick Read: ***Stay out of your own way!***

• As much as careful planning can help you attain your goal, it can create extra burdens and problems in your life. This is not the time to be overly analytical—in other words, don't make the mistake of overthinking things during the planning stages. Keep good records and make comprehensive lists, but don't be too bogged down by details or you are likely to be disappointed by the results.

• Nagging and bickering can become a source of aggravation between you and a partner or colleague, even if the two of you happen to be on the same page. Whenever possible, avoid a tendency to blame and find fault. Too much criticism can undermine a relationship, as well as your own belief in yourself. Once you start questioning that, you might as well say good-bye to the pleasure or success of your project.

Secret: Things are in flux; you should not attempt to make too many plans for the future at this time. Let one change lead naturally to the next, rather than trying to make things happen according to plan. You'll regret it if you do.

Three of Wands

KEYWORDS

• *Opportunity* • *Enjoyment* • *Advantage* • *Innovation* • *Prospect* • *Union*

UPRIGHT

Quick Read: ***Opportunities abound.***

• You are entering a blithe and happy time when countless chances for success exist. These may be even more than you are aware of, but you must be careful not to let them slip away. Allow yourself to feel happy and fortunate without questioning why this is happening. Now it is time to sow the seeds of future harvests. Be excited by your good fortune and realize that you are the architect. Almost unlimited success awaits you in the future, so long as you have the grit to pursue it. If you need a little help, don't be afraid to use your connections or call in some favors.

• Don't expect all of these chances to come to you in the usual, predictable fashion. They may come virtually out of the blue. Be awake and aware to all the possibilities open to you at this time. A friend or partner may have a great suggestion that will inspire you to take a risk or two, so be open to it. Remember, if you are smart, open-minded, and willing to cooperate, you will be sure to get your wish.

Secret: Embrace the unknown! Many of your best opportunities are likely to come in the guise of something else. So long as you are alert, flexible, and in tune with the importance of cooperation, you will get a chance to shine.

REVERSED

Quick Read: ***Seize the day.***

• In the past, you may have allowed some important opportunities to pass you by, simply because you weren't able to recognize them. Moreover, you might have followed the advice of others instead of trusting your own path to success. Believe it or not, there can be drawbacks to good luck, especially if you aren't motivated to do some of the work yourself.

• This card reversed can also represent a marvelous opportunity squandered out of foolish or reckless behavior. It is possible that you are currently basking in lazy anticipation of more good luck coming your way, to the point where you can't choose the best time to go for it. Another possibility is that you have a passive attitude that kills your chances to succeed.

Secret: This is not the time to be lazy. You might feel as if there are so many good influences in your life right now that you don't need to push your luck, but that is a mistake. Do not ignore good prospects.

Four of Wands

KEYWORDS

• Harmony • Completion • Foundation • Stability • Equilibrium • Appreciation

UPRIGHT

Quick Read: ***Count your blessings.***

• Currently you are surrounded by an aura of optimism. You feel supported, validated, and justly proud of a job well done. Not only do the feelings themselves elevate you, but the work you have done has built a foundation for the future.

• Give a party. Whether it is to mark the end of a specific project or just to observe a general happiness in your life, you deserve to rejoice. It is likely that an important date, such as a wedding, anniversary, or birthday, is coming up in the near future, and nothing makes you quite so happy as getting together with friends, family, and other loved ones to celebrate. Part of the reason you worked so hard in the past was to get to this point in your life, where you can feel good about all you have managed to accomplish, sometimes against considerable odds.

Secret: Even if you are comfortable in your current course of action, you may worry about losing the foundation that you have worked so hard to attain. You need to trust more fully in the good fortune and good karma you've created. Give thanks.

REVERSED

Quick Read: ***Try to forgive and forget.***

• This is a time in your life when you need to let go of anger and resentments that may be buried inside, due to plans that didn't work out. If someone has let you down, you need to forgive, forget, and get on with your life. Naturally, it is common to sulk and even hatch plans for revenge when you feel as if someone you care about has let you down. That sort of attitude only leads to unhappiness and greater problems in the future. Also, it is important to keep in mind that negative thoughts and compulsive behavior can interfere with trust and commitment.

• Don't spend too much time puzzling over why a friend or friends have not come through for you in the wake of a recent disappointment. That merely takes time away from the effort required to get to work on something more productive.

Secret: Try to let go of resentments and complaining. Take comfort in the knowledge that unexpected turns in the road can be rewarding in ways that are not apparent now. It may be a time of instability or disharmony on the home front.

Five of Wands

KEYWORDS

• Competition • Struggle • Challenge • Contest • Obstacles • Antagonism

UPRIGHT

Quick Read: ***Stand up for yourself.***

• This card not only foretells conflict, but also predicts that it is time for you to explore just what a competitive spirit means and to use it in a way that demonstrates tolerance and respect for your opponent. Your challenge is to turn your current battleground into a home-field advantage. You can do this without being a bully or even being openly aggressive. Simply present yourself as a worthy opponent who knows how to stand up for his or her convictions while showing tolerance for the opposing side.

• Balancing an attitude of fairness with a desire to stand up for your own point of view can be tough, but when you do, you feel invigorated, not defeated by the conflict. Also, you may be able to learn something valuable from your opponent. This is a period when you need to understand just what true competition requires.

Secret: Refuse to be a victim! Even if once in a while you lose a round or two, don't let a temporary defeat injure your self-confidence. You are stronger than that. Rise to the challenge at hand and defend your position. Compromise may eventually be in order.

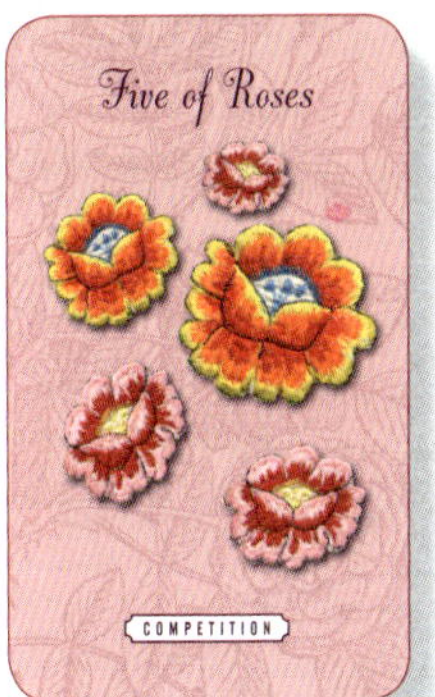

REVERSED

Quick Read: ***Don't make it personal.***

• Even if you currently find yourself in a fight with high stakes, keep the contest on a civil, elevated level. You should never allow this intense rivalry to degenerate into a shallow contest of egos where the question becomes "Who is right?" instead of "What is right?" The Five of Wands reversed suggests that you take any competition much too personally now. You might just want to win and be right about something, which doesn't mean that you are. Alternatively, you could take the exact opposite approach, being too meek to fight for what you want simply because you're afraid you won't win.

• Stress can be a major issue for you now, especially if you aren't competitive by nature. This can be complicated by the fact that there may be unsavory or untrue rumors circulating about you. Be careful that you don't jump to conclusions. It is possible that the information wasn't spread by the source you thought, and if you get angry you will only create a more difficult situation.

Secret: You need to guard against an attitude of frustration, anger, or revenge. Fighting for something you believe in doesn't mean that you have to give up your civility. You will lose respect for yourself if you do.

Six of Wands

KEYWORDS

• Victory • Applause
• Approval • Endorsement
• Transcendence
• Adjustments

UPRIGHT

Quick Read: ***V is for victory!***

• It is no wonder that you feel like a winner—you are one! The spotlight is on you at this time, indicating a gratifying period in your life. With so much energy and excitement at your disposal, you are charged with charisma and eager to make important decisions about your future. You should use a current victory to build a foundation for future successes.

• You also need to realize that just because everything is going your way now does not mean that it will do so forever. Therefore, enjoy your success while it is at hand, and do not take it for granted. If you are merely on the brink of a new victory, you can presume that the outcome will turn out positively for you. When that victory comes, you need to accept the time of recognition as something you deserve and have worked hard to attain.

Secret: In the future, whenever you face a time of crisis, be certain to remember this period when you won and everything was going your way. You will realize that a positive attitude had a great deal to do with your success.

REVERSED

Quick Read: ***Beware of phonies.***

• Because you may be unsure of exactly what you want at this time, you might be conflicted about what comes your way. It is likely that you have an inflated opinion of yourself at this moment, feeling as if you deserve a great deal more than you actually do. It is possible that you have one or more flatterers in your circle, and they are also responsible for turning your head and making you believe that you are more exceptional than you are. You shouldn't let these people influence your self-evaluation but should work hard to be deserving of a victory.

• Keep in mind that you are unlikely to receive the rewards that you deserve so long as your number one thought is your own needs and illusions of grandeur. That attitude will only narrow your focus and make it impossible for you to accomplish the victories that you really want.

Secret: In the past you took advantage of the victories that came your way, but it inflated your ego. You may not have learned that in order to be worthwhile, the credit for success needs to be shared with your closest friends and allies.

Seven of Wands

KEYWORDS

• *Determination* • *Bravery* • *Character* • *Daring* • *Commitment* • *Valor*

UPRIGHT

Quick Read: ***Defend your beliefs.***

• This card represents a time in your life when you are sure to be challenged to defend your personal beliefs and values. Don't expect it to be easy. This task requires a great deal of backbone, and you will have to be amazingly assertive in order to win the day. Defend the values that you love. Don't be tempted to compromise your position on important issues, because it is never worth it. If you must fight on your own, without allies, you can still win, so long as you have determination and faith in what you are doing.

• You may wonder if it is cowardly to be afraid in this situation, but be assured that it isn't. What distinguishes a hero from a coward is that the hero fights on despite fear. Let that thought guide you in this hour, and you will have the strength, endurance, and shrewdness that your situation requires.

Secret: You need to dig deep into your psyche to find your spiritual strength. Understand how assertiveness and spirituality can be balanced to create the commitment you need now. They can be a formidable combination in your character.

REVERSED

Quick Read: ***Fear is the enemy.***

• The Seven of Wands reversed can signal that it may be difficult for you to fight off your worst fears. You may feel overwhelmed by challenging circumstances, and in such a case it can seem easier to retreat rather than stand up to what you fear is coming. Hurt and abandonment issues are likely to come to the surface now, making you feel as if you have been neglected or betrayed by someone you love very dearly. If you and a mate are truly at odds, you are likely to take a defensive position, unwilling to give so much as an inch, yet this is not a time to assert yourself so blatantly.

• Being afraid can create an atmosphere of panic and doubt, making you question yourself about nearly everything and making you fearful of trying something new. Even though going it alone may be exactly what you should do now, you probably fear that solution as well.

Secret: This card can indicate a willingness to give up on a relationship or an individual because you are afraid of commitment. Ask yourself this question first: Is love stronger than fear? Find ways to deal with your feelings of fight or flight.

Eight of Wands

KEYWORDS

• Gallantry • Hope
• Signals • Innovation
• Communication
• Messages

UPRIGHT

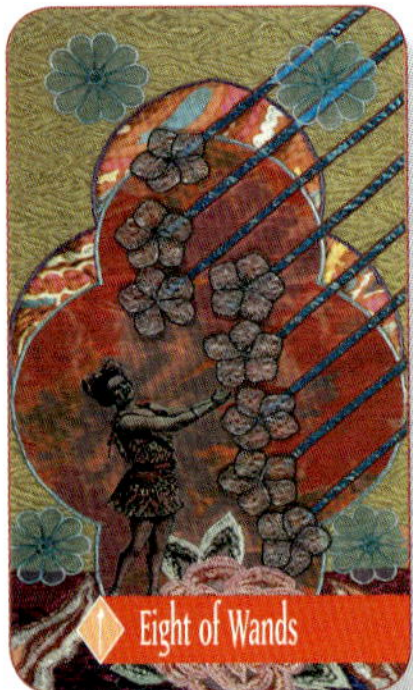

Quick Read: ***Take action now!***

• Whatever it is, there is no time to waste. Do it and do it now. It is best that you communicate your intentions clearly and with force. Show that you are someone who knows how important it is for all of your intentions, both romantic and platonic, to be fully expressed and understood before any action is taken. Wasting time is the worst thing you can do now, but miscommunicating your intentions comes a close second.

• You may be feeling exceptionally tuned-in to a wonderful person at this time. In order to make this relationship (whether it be romance, friendship, or creative partnership) work, you need to be totally honest about your feelings. Don't expect the other person to read your mind. Even if verbal communication isn't your thing, make an effort to speak your mind. Be clear, concise, and to the point.

Secret: There is such a thing as waiting too long to put plans into operation. Don't make that mistake, because the energy generated on your behalf by the universe will be this powerful for only a short time. Send a message of love!

REVERSED

Quick Read: ***Avoid a failure to communicate.***

• It isn't easy to get your message out to others now, for one reason or another. Plus, directions are likely to go awry; sentiments can be misinterpreted or even ignored altogether. You might experience problems relating to communication channels such as phones, computers, or even the mail. Alternatively, you could find yourself emotionally tongue-tied, unable to speak the words that express how you really feel inside.

• Where relationships are concerned, the Eight of Wands reversed can mean that you will soon discover that someone for whom you have strong feelings does not return the sentiment. It is also possible that this individual has been deliberately stringing you along, trying to make you believe in a relationship that can never be what you expect or want it to be. You might even wonder if the other person ever cared for you at all or meant the endearments that were spoken. That can hurt, so beware.

Secret: You may decide to reveal a special secret to a friend or mate, believing it will have a powerful effect on this person. Alas, the time has passed for the news to have any power. Be careful of a betrayal of confidence.

Nine of Wands

KEYWORDS

• Discipline • Guard
• Preparedness
• Faithfulness • Endurance
• Restrictions

UPRIGHT

Quick Read: ***Discipline is the key.***

• Discipline and strength of character are your best weapons now. Your willpower is soon to be tested, and in order to come out successfully on the other side of that challenge, you must apply techniques of strict military-style discipline to your behavior. Because this card could also represent a physical challenge in the making, it is important that you keep your body strong and healthy by exercising and eating right.

• You have a core of strength inside you, perhaps even greater than you realize. Because of this you can discipline yourself to do what must be done. Don't do anything to excess or you will regret it. Stay away from people who give off a negative vibe, people who drink to the point of drunkenness, or people who are addicted to drugs. Naturally, you should avoid these excesses yourself.

Secret: Visualizing yourself as a member of the military can actually help you to follow through on a challenging task of endurance. If you believe you have no choice but to follow an order, you are more likely to obey.

REVERSED

Quick Read: ***Find a happy medium.***

• This card reversed can be a tough influence because it signals a tendency for extremism. Either you are not willing to sacrifice self-indulgent pleasures or you are much too rigid in the way you discipline or deny yourself. You have the potential to find the middle road between the two extremes, but stubbornness or a lack of restraint could be blocking your path. Don't expect one strict set of rules to cover every endeavor or circumstance. Beware of letting someone convince you to get involved in an endeavor that goes against your better nature.

• There is also a possibility that at this time you may be inclined to stay with an individual who doesn't treat you well, even though you feel that the relationship has lost its luster. Alternatively, you might give up on a relationship too soon. The feeling that you must discipline your actions is very strong in you, so if you fall short of the mark you have set for yourself, you are likely to be disappointed, no matter what the result might be.

Secret: It is easy for you to allow yourself to be taken advantage of during this period. Perhaps you know better, but someone you love or admire might make you feel ungrateful if you try to be independent. Don't be influenced in an unhealthy way.

Ten of Wands

KEYWORDS

• Oppression • Burden • Overwork • Desperation • Distractions • Exhaustion

UPRIGHT

Quick Read: ***Pace yourself.***

• You need to stop working so hard. Forces of oppression—perhaps of your own making—currently surround you, and they are asking more than you are able to give. If you have over-committed yourself, chances are that everything feels like a huge bother. The resulting fatigue and discouragement can drain you of physical and spiritual energy, leaving you unable to express your creative potential. You might believe that the more projects you take on, the more successful you will be. Instead, you are only siphoning off your precious resources.

• Take time to think through your predicament, guided by common sense, not ego. You simply cannot do everything you want to now. Try sharing your concern and worries with a mentor or adviser. You need to learn ways to conserve energy between projects. Pace yourself whenever it is possible. There is nothing wrong with having lots of irons in the fire, but if you make it a contest, you will end up being the loser.

Secret: Learn to identify whether or not you are a workaholic. If you bend all of your energy toward work instead of personal relationships, you probably are. It is time to bring more balance into your life. Take a time-out.

REVERSED

Quick Read: ***Define your goals.***

• Unless you have a clear idea of where you want to go in life, you are going to go on working yourself into the ground with no good results to show for it. Even if you realize that you need to make some major changes, you might feel emotionally impotent, unable to act in your own best interests, overwhelmed by the many commitments you have made.

• When the Ten of Wands is reversed, it usually means that you are expecting too much of yourself, yet resenting the demands that are being made on you. You might feel like a martyr, bogged down by family responsibilities and professional demands you can't possibly satisfy. Yet even though you feel alone with your burdens, it is unlikely that you will reach out to the people you love and trust. Clearly, you are not able to make good, clear decisions at this time.

Secret: A pattern from your past could be influencing your relationships in a negative way. A controlling attitude may have made you too rigid and opinionated. Find ways to dig down deep into your psyche. Don't be a victim.

Princess (or Page) of Wands

KEYWORDS

• Spontaneity • Impatience • Enthusiasm • Liberality • Innocence • Youthfulness

UPRIGHT

Quick Read: *Go for it!*

• This card denotes a period when you either embody youth and excitement or are under the influence of someone who fits that description. There is a difficult balancing act between showing your rash, wild side and tempering it with a steadier, more mature attitude. If a relationship is in the offing, you need to be sure that you are not getting involved with someone who either is too young for you or acts in an overly rebellious, immature, or reckless manner.

• One of the trends going for you right now is your unfettered belief that wonderful things are about to happen. Your youthful, appealing, and romantic spirit is certain to captivate those around you. People are charmed by your spontaneous and unstudied exuberance and are likely to respond to you in kind. You bring enthusiasm and excitement to everything you do.

Secret: If you feel you are jumping headfirst into a situation, do your best to stay composed. Don't allow your impetuous nature to turn into impatience or irritation, because that will only keep you from achieving a goal.

REVERSED

Quick Read: *Act your age.*

• One of the hallmarks of youth is immaturity. This may describe you, someone who is part of your life now, or someone who is about to join your circle. You may have to deal with the characteristic recklessness of a young person or put up with an immature friend's antics. Whether or not these traits are a part of your own character, you need to beware of being annoying, speaking carelessly, or being hotheaded.

• A lack of spontaneity or eagerness can be equally self-defeating. There is no shame in being inexperienced, so long as you are open to gaining wisdom and experience in whatever way the universe sees fit to bestow it. Your challenge at this time is to keep from appearing as if you are indiscreet, imprudent, or foolish. This means you need to refrain from spreading gossip or rumors of any kind. Be more aware of developing your social skills. By the same token, beware of doing too much socializing, especially with people who don't really matter to you.

Secret: Exemplify what is best about whatever age you are. If you are an adult, act like one. If you are young, don't pretend that you have all the answers. Do your best to balance the innocence of youth with the wisdom of years.

Prince (or Knight) of Wands

KEYWORDS
- *Ambition* • *Passion*
- *Impetuousness*
- *Progress* • *Quarrels*
- *Movement*

UPRIGHT

Quick Read: ***Move forward.***

• It is time to come out of your shell, to explore your chances in the wider, more expansive vistas of the world. There is a possibility of a change of residence or a new job. Whether you realize it or not, you are searching for ways to expand your experience. Passion and a fearless desire to take risks will be your guides.

• You are surrounded by ambition, and your motivation to advance and move closer to your goals is very strong at this time, yet you should guard against boasting too much about your present aspirations or past successes. Don't waste time looking back. Your future beckons. If there is someone in your life who displays the characteristics of the Prince of Wands, you may feel slightly overwhelmed or overshadowed by this person's power—yet you cannot help falling under his or her charismatic spell.

Secret: Don't deny who you are; don't be afraid to show that you are a unique entity. Be proud of yourself, where you came from, and where you are going. See yourself as a virtual pioneer, an explorer. A move might be indicated.

REVERSED

Quick Read: ***Be careful. Don't make a move you will regret.***

• This card can reflect an unsettled, quarrelsome period for you, especially if you feel that an individual who is important to you is in some way trying to hold you back. Ambition can be a useful tool in helping you get ahead, but at this point your blind ambition could be your ultimate undoing. A tendency to try to improve someone for his or her own good is a bad idea now.

• The Prince of Wands reversed can signal that an individual with his characteristics is currently exacting too much influence over you. Be aware of your own ambitions to succeed, and don't seek to emulate the accomplishments or drive of others. That is a mistake. If you represent these traits, you may appear overly domineering and quarrelsome to the people you deal with on a regular basis. Where a romantic possibility exists, avoid getting involved too quickly or becoming entangled with an individual who is more ego than substance.

Secret: You should try not to fight over changing your job or residence. Don't stay rooted in a career or even a city that you feel doesn't work for you anymore. A lack of ambition merely wastes your time.

Queen of Wands

KEYWORDS
- *Inspiration* • *Energy*
- *Goals* • *Confidence*
- *Sociability* • *Pride*

UPRIGHT

Quick Read: ***Assert yourself.***

• Whether or not you possess the characteristics suggested by this card, you need to start behaving as if you do! If you act confident or socially self-assured, people will automatically treat you as if you *are*. Creative and inspired projects are looming in the near future, so you would be wise to turn the majority of your talent and ambition in their direction. Attending parties can be more useful than any business meetings now.

• If you are not the person described by this card, it is likely that someone very much in her image will soon enter your life. As a romantic partner, she could be the love of your life. As a friend, boss, mentor, or colleague, she can be a great force for encouragement and resources. Perhaps, by emulating her bold behavior and royal air, you will be able to tap into your own unique gifts, showing off your magnetic personality and captivating intelligence. Use the connections you have to make the connections you want.

Secret: Use your anger as a tool, not a weapon. Instead of becoming frustrated and upset, put your emotions to good use by letting them inspire and motivate you. A good leader is a good example. Channel your energy into creative outlets.

REVERSED

Quick Read: ***Waste not, want not.***

• Even if you have all the potential in the world, it won't do you any good if you don't use it correctly or to your benefit. The Queen of Wands reversed sometimes indicates that you are using your charm in a negative or cajoling way. Just because you *can* walk between the raindrops doesn't mean that you should. If you want to be thought of as a leader, don't make the mistake of being bossy or overly demanding. People will follow you because you inspire their respect and loyalty and not because you know what buttons to push. Behaving in such a way does a disservice to the gifts that God/Goddess has showered on you.

• It is also possible that someone who is charismatic and commanding has been exerting a powerful effect on you, but she is to be avoided if she is narcissistic and manipulative. She will hinder—not help—you, despite the great attraction and admiration you may feel for her.

Secret: Be prepared, not passive. At times, creative ideas can lull you into a state of laziness and emotional torpor or empty socializing. Remember that artistic temperament, talent, and great connections are worthless unless they are backed up by hard work.

King of Wands

KEYWORDS

- *Dynamism* • *Actions*
- *Idealism* • *Keenness*
- *Analysis* • *Leadership*

UPRIGHT

Quick Read: *Just do it.*

• This is an opportunity to take strong, dynamic action in order to reach your most cherished goals. Let others know that you mean business. Reward loyalty, but punish those who deserve to be punished. Only by showing that you are in charge can you prove to those around you—especially those who work for you—who is boss.

• Your actions are the key to how others perceive you. If you envision yourself as forceful, firm, and dominant, then that is the vibe you'll give off. Don't doubt yourself, and don't show fear, even if you are afraid. If you do not fit these criteria, it is likely that you will soon meet or be influenced by an individual of this type. This is someone you may want to emulate. If you do, you are certain to become a more fiery and self-confident person.

Secret: Confront your greatest strengths and weaknesses. Make a list of them and study your list with an objective eye. Only by being absolutely true to yourself can you gain the self-knowledge needed to improve your life. Then take action!

REVERSED

Quick Read: *Beware of distractions.*

• Because you have so many projects going on now, it is impossible to give enough attention to each of them. As a result, you may not be able to handle any one endeavor to the best of your ability. When the King of Wands is reversed, it can mean that you are ready to rush into a situation impetuously and perhaps without all the facts in hand. Though you may be confident that your actions are valid, you should not be so headstrong that you can't see things from a different point of view.

• You may have recently become involved with an individual who has the characteristics of the King of Wands. This has not been a happy partnership, however, because he has demonstrated that he may be showing a false face. This can indicate a person who is too bossy and likes to talk about himself a great deal while showing little concern for others. Needless to say, if you currently embody any of these characteristics, some changes should be made!

Secret: Stay away from gambling because you are not likely to be lucky. Worst of all, you could be going through an arrogant, rebellious phase that makes you feel as if you can do anything you please. Don't be a show-off.

SWORDS

(also known as Air, Spades, Blades, or Wings)

Ace of Swords

KEYWORDS

• *Triumph* • *Concentration* • *Brilliance* • *Uniqueness* • *Force* • *Purpose*

UPRIGHT

Quick Read: ***Concentration is the key.***

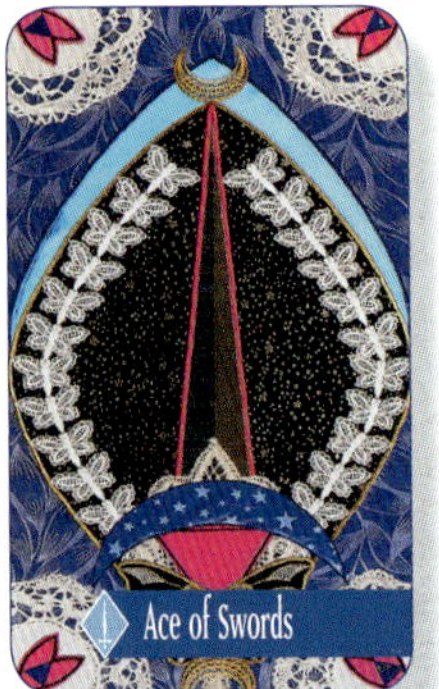

• This card can be read as representing a two-edged sword, suggesting both attack and defense. Even though in the main the influence is positive, you could find yourself pushing too many new ideas or trying to achieve too many goals at the same time. It is best if you become single-minded and focused on one point to be successful. By concentrating your attention, you will open up a channel to deep and profound ideas.

• At this time you are determined to triumph over lies, adversity, and ignorance. Standing up for dearly held principles can help you make your mark. Best of all, you are able to cut through illusions that may have clouded your judgment in the past. You know the value of chopping away the old, dead wood in order to make room for new growth and new beginnings. Only by doing this can you expect your unique plan or strategy to come to fruition.

Secret: It is good to cut to the chase by presenting your plan in a clear and precise manner. It is easy to see yourself as the embodiment of an important new goal or life principle, yet if you push too hard there may be push-back from others. Stand up for your ideas, but don't force them.

REVERSED

Quick Read: ***Don't be so pushy!***

• You believe firmly in your course of action, and that is good. If you refuse to admit new information or to allow opposing views to have a voice, though, you are not operating according to the universe's plan. Moreover, if you use your intellect and knowledge as weapons to compel things to go a certain way, you can be sure the plan will backfire. You also need to be realistic in what you expect from a mate, friend, or close associate. If you set the bar too high, you are sure to be disillusioned at some point.

• Beware of instituting a self-fulfilling prophecy. For instance, if you fear that you or someone close to you is not up to a challenge, you are virtually giving such a negative thought the power to come true. If you are not sure about speaking your mind because of how your words will be received, keep silent.

Secret: You should never follow any plan, goal, or individual with blind obedience. Having doubts, even in the face of admiration, is not only reasonable but healthy. Question what someone is trying forcefully to convince you of.

Two of Swords

KEYWORDS

- Balance • Alternatives
- Rest • Withdrawal
- Diplomacy
- Compromise

UPRIGHT

Quick Read: ***Balance work and play.***

• It is time for you to start looking at things from another's point of view. While you shouldn't toss out your most cherished opinions, you should be willing to give them a second look. There is a likelihood that you will want to share opinions with others, but neither you nor those in your circle should be dogmatic or stubborn about your views. Perhaps you realize that being right is not nearly as important as being kind and fair.

• Compromise doesn't mean surrender, but it is a delicate line to walk. Although you need to take a break from your usual way of thinking and toying with new concepts, give yourself permission to dream and look within yourself for answers. People change, and it is possible that you have altered your views considerably in recent months. It is a good time to regroup and get balanced.

Secret: Take a vacation, or at least get some rest. Overworking yourself, either physically or mentally, can lead to frustration and fatigue. Plus, it can have an inhibitive effect on the way you make decisions. Clear your mind and breathe.

REVERSED

Quick Read: ***Procrastination and postponements threaten.***

• You may feel as if you've been swallowed up by a fog, unable to navigate through a current problem. Your ideas and opinions have probably changed recently, but much of your motivation also may have vanished. Taking too much time out from important matters can block your forward motion. It is possible that what began as a break could have turned into a habit of procrastinating. Because of this you find yourself equivocating over just about every challenge or decision you face now—big or small.

• Where a relationship is concerned, you are likely to be in limbo. Worrying about whether or not you should declare your feelings to a new love interest could create problems for you now. However, you must also guard against getting involved in a questionable relationship. You may not have all the pieces of the puzzle right now, so for the time being, you are probably wise to let things remain as they are.

Secret: Be careful what people you associate with during this period because you are easily influenced now. Someone who is shallow or otherwise unworthy of your company may be a drain on your emotional and spiritual energy. Stop procrastinating.

Three of Swords

KEYWORDS
• Sorrow • Pain
• Disappointment
• Recovery • Regret
• Healing

UPRIGHT

Quick Read: ***Sorrow is a part of life.***

• Despite your best efforts and expectations, there are times when life can be hurtful. Your heart may be feeling heavy with sadness. It maybe that past hurts are resurfacing because an incident has scratched an old wound. Denying that you are experiencing great emotional suffering at this time won't do you any good—in fact, such denial can lead to hostility and even illness. So, although sorrow itself can block progress, pretending that it doesn't exist draws out the process even longer.

• This is a period when you finally need to come to terms with a deeply held sadness or a broken heart. As hard as it can be to do this, you need to keep in mind that healing can begin only after the pain has been acknowledged and accepted. Yes, your defenses are down, but once you allow yourself to lower your expectations, you can begin to make peace with the past.

Secret: In order to recover from emotional pain, you must court faith, forgiveness, and self-love. Do not doubt your inner strength now, no matter how lost you may feel. Take time to count your blessings—you have more than you realize.

REVERSED

Quick Read: ***Care, but don't be careless.***

• There is no way around it—before you can expect to be happy again, you need to feel helpless, sorrowful, and despairing. It is a difficult and unpleasant process, but you must face it. Remember the old saying "Whatever doesn't kill you makes you stronger." If the sorrow represents someone else's suffering—that of a person you love dearly—it could be even more of a trial, since you will feel helpless and weak.

• It is a mistake to hide your feelings from others, especially those close to you. If you do, you will appear phony and insincere. If you shoulder your pain without seeming to wallow in self-pity, you will receive compassion. Be careful of irrational behavior, either in yourself or in others. You could appear to be cold and manipulative now. Personal hardship can make it tough for you to treat others with the courtesy and consideration they deserve. Professional counseling may be the answer to your problems.

Secret: Think twice before you take on the role of caregiver, either physical or emotional, to anyone at this time. Your sense of empathy is strong, but your motives could be misguided, born out of a need to feel needed. It is OK to take care of yourself.

Four of Swords

KEYWORDS
- Seclusion • Awareness
- Relaxation • Strategy
- Meditation • Retreat

UPRIGHT

Quick Read: ***Make a strategic withdrawal.***

• During this period, you need to take a break from life's pressures and demands, especially in your social life. A situation that concerns you at the present time requires seclusion in order for you to divest yourself of anxiety and stress. Even if you don't realize it, you need a real spiritual change of scene. Try to meditate or pray every day. This will help you find your emotional center, and you will feel far less vulnerable and fearful as a result.

• You need to take time out to reflect on your life and your beliefs, and by doing this you will be refreshed and renewed. Pay attention to your inner life. When negative thoughts intrude, notice them as if from a distance, and then imagine that you are watching them go, disappearing like a puff of smoke. If you practice this exercise for a few minutes every day, you will become more calm and focused.

Secret: If you are looking for love or contentment, you are most likely to find it in quiet, healing places and with gentle, spiritually aware people. Casual affairs or superficial people cannot give you the stability and sensitivity you need at this point in your life.

REVERSED

Quick Read: ***Avoid confrontation.***

• It would be a mistake to get into a battle of wills now, because you simply don't have the stomach for it. Instead, this is a time to retreat in the midst of what appears to be disturbing turmoil and chaos. Take time to examine your thoughts without distractions. Take sanctuary where you can find it. Don't allow yourself to be drawn into controversy now or to be ruled by someone's selfish demands. Instead, you need to court tranquility.

• At this time, you are probably feeling stressed, emotionally drained by upsets and negative external influences. To rid yourself of this anxiety, you need to center and ground yourself. It is possible that you have been retreating from issues that should have been faced years ago. Now you have come to the point where you must make peace with your issues, and the best way to approach this is with a strategy of inner peace and harmony.

Secret: If you get quiet and shut out distractions, you will recharge your inner strength. During this period, problems in a relationship could be the result of apprehension that if you open your heart fully, you will be hurt. Learn to trust again. Take time out, but don't run away.

Five of Swords

KEYWORDS

• Defeat • Anger
• Problems • Distress
• Lesson • Dissatisfaction

UPRIGHT

Quick Read: ***Learn from your mistakes.***

• There are times in life when victory is simply impossible and defeat must be accepted. This is one of those times. Alternatively, you may win, but it takes so much out of you that you feel you've lost. This is called a "hollow victory." If possible, try to put this in a positive light by looking at defeat as a lesson that can ensure future success.

• Yes, you are in a complicated situation now, but letting go of something that is important to you should not make you feel or behave like a victim. Try to be more analytical. There may be times when you feel as if you are never going to move beyond the current defeat, but the real defeat is in not learning from the mistakes of the past.

Secret: Be prepared for some people to revel in your apparent failure. It isn't fair, but they may even believe that you got what was coming to you. Ultimately, the only opinion that matters is yours. Remember, if you're not failing, you're not trying!

REVERSED

Quick Read: ***Don't be a sore loser!***

• We live in a highly competitive world, and because of this it can be easy to forget that not all battles can be won. Every once in a while, surrender is necessary. Attitude is everything when going through a phase like this, so be honest about what you are experiencing. Don't strike a pose of false victory that you can exploit to others. It's false, it's dishonest, and it won't work.

• Defeat blocks progress, and having the attitude of a loser guarantees loss in the future. Examine your past and analyze your behavior at that time. If past lessons were ignored, you will probably experience a loss again. The truth is that you cannot cheat karma. You will reap what you sow. Own your behavior or change your attitude. Show the universe that you can learn a lesson, benefiting from the current defeat and sadness in which you find yourself mired.

Secret: This is not the time to divulge an embarrassing secret. You may think that by revealing somebody else's dirty laundry, you are making things better for yourself, but that is not the case. Beware of your envy of another's victory. It does not become you.

Six of Swords

KEYWORDS

• Passage • Transition
• Beliefs • Improvement
• Resolution • Renewal

UPRIGHT

Quick Read: ***You've weathered the storm.***

• You are emerging from a difficult and demanding time, preparing to shake off what you have been through. Now you are about to enter a time of peace, contentment, and happiness. You feel and believe that a change of direction offers you a whole new perspective on life. It is great to know that you will see an improvement. You have made the passage, you have endured a hard transition, and now you are ready to take on demands with a renewed attitude.

• Travel plans could figure in your future. This helps you put the changes in your life into perspective. By defying your orderly view of things, including your schedule, you will be able to prepare yourself for the changes to come. Do your best to visualize the challenges in your life as doors that you can open to reveal rich and exciting rewards.

Secret: You should not be afraid of a test or challenge. In recent months you have "studied" for just such a thing. You have been through a lot and are stronger and more decisive than you realize, so embrace challenges with joy and eagerness.

REVERSED

Quick Read: ***Try to stay calm.***

• A patient and focused approach is what you need now in order to get through any problems that might threaten to get you off track. Even though you have benefited from a recent transition in your life, you may feel insecure, threatened by passing from one stage to another. Your mind could be occupied by a past test that may not have been successful.

• You may have trouble maintaining a positive attitude because of your fear that you won't be able to measure up to what is expected of you. You need to understand that if you can change your mind, you can change your life. Don't give up simply because you are afraid of life's challenges. Your transition—both personal and in other avenues of your life—can be a positive demonstration of how your changing beliefs have influenced your life. They might take a little growing into, but with patience and time, you can make it happen.

Secret: The negativity in your midst may not be your own. It is possible that someone important to you or with whom you spend a lot of time is creating a toxic atmosphere due to negative thoughts and comments. It may be time to calmly move on.

Seven of Swords

KEYWORDS

• Opposition • Failure
• Negativity • Priorities
• Odds • Enemy

UPRIGHT

Quick Read: ***Ward off negativity.***

• It is time for you to learn how to make opposition work to your benefit. While this isn't necessarily an easy concept to adopt, you will be better off once you have mastered it. There are people waiting to bring you down, and if you aren't careful, they will succeed. No amount of grandstanding or rash behavior is going to stop it from happening. Instead, let logic and subtlety, not manipulation, be your guides.

• Whether or not you are willing to accept the fact, someone you know or work with could be marshaling forces against you. This may sound dramatic, but the fact is that you do not fully appreciate the extent of the power operating against you. The best way to help combat this is to visualize yourself in the position of those who oppose you. Imagine their power, and use it.

Secret: A great deal of the opposition you are currently encountering is self-created. Once you can accept that fact, you are on the road to solving the problem. Let others see that you are neither afraid nor timid. Stay positive. Don't use trickery.

REVERSED

Quick Read: ***Evaluate your opposition.***

• Opposition always blocks progress, especially if you are a part of the problem! If others are or have been deceiving you, you won't improve matters by acting in the same way. It is possible that in the past you managed to acquire a lot of negative energy and it is just waiting to take you down. You should not discount the overwhelming power of this force by minimizing its effect, because it can be toxic.

• If at this time you are feeling alone or restricted, things will only get worse for you because inertia fuels a negative self-image. Don't berate yourself, but don't gloss over your faults, either. If you feel it will help, make a list of traits you need to enhance and others that you need to play down. There may be a tendency to use deceit or trickery in order to get what you want, but don't go down that path. You will be sorry if you do.

Secret: Are you your own worst enemy? This is a question worth asking yourself now. Don't be afraid to stand up for yourself, but don't play a deceitful game. You should not doubt your ability to reform. Consider the vibes you are sending out to others—positive or negative?

Eight of Swords

KEYWORDS

• *Indecision* • *Pettiness* • *Helplessness* • *Misunderstanding* • *Warning* • *Inertia*

UPRIGHT

Quick Read: ***Don't decide yet.***

• In times of doubt and confusion, such as you may be experiencing now, don't be afraid to delay your actions. Take your time. Look patiently within yourself for answers. Your higher mind knows what to do. No one else can help you achieve clarity. Don't overanalyze your current predicament or expect someone else to come to your rescue. This is something only you can fix, but sometimes it is good not to make a quick decision.

• If you are accustomed to being decisive, it can be hard for you to put on the brakes now. You may worry that you have lost your edge and that if you wait too long, a chance might be missed. Whether or not that is true, you need to take the philosophical approach. Be patient. The result will be worth the wait.

Secret: In the past, a lack of perspective or a rash act may have crippled your faith, making it hard for you to see things realistically. Now you need to avoid misunderstandings. Gather information before deciding. If you feel confused, maybe a wise counselor can help.

REVERSED

Quick Read: ***Indecision will cause problems.***

• This is not a good time to be around negative, emotionally toxic people. If their influence is strong, it could cause you to make improper, even foolish decisions. This is particularly true if the person in question is your mate, a family member, or a close associate. You should not allow love or familial closeness to obscure the truth. Indecision can make you feel hopeless, alone, and confused, but simply choosing the lesser of two evils isn't going to get you out of your difficulties, either.

• There are times when it is best to decide *not* to decide. However, if it is absolutely vital that a decision be made, gather as much information as you can and then consult an oracle. This may be your own subconscious or some other esoteric method of divination such as the Tarot itself. Expect your inner voice to speak to you through a dream. Prayer and meditation help you to channel the truth.

Secret: Nothing is happening now, and you may feel as if this lack of action is driving you crazy. Take a Zen-like approach by opening your mind to what the universe wants for you. The answer will come. Slow down—this, too, shall pass.

Nine of Swords

KEYWORDS

• *Nightmare* • *Obsession* • *Anxiety* • *Insomnia* • *Dark side* • *Martyr*

UPRIGHT

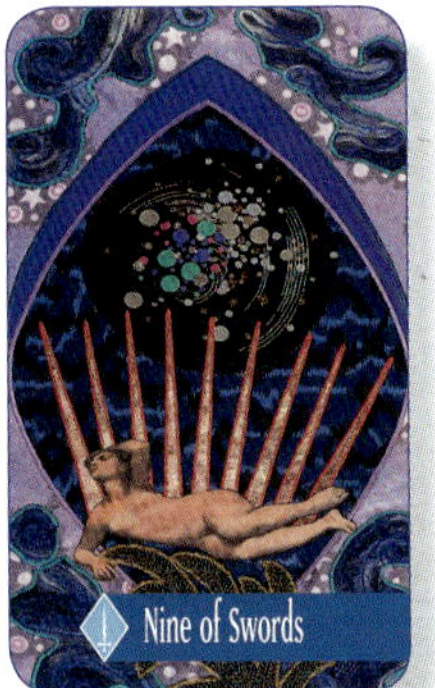

Quick Read: ***What are you obsessing about?***

• This card signals a struggle with obsession, perhaps even insomnia. You must confront your worst fears and overcome any cynicism in your own nature. Those fears, left ignored and unresolved, can lead to paranoia or even physical indisposition. Past uncertainties are affecting your present situation, making it hard or even impossible to keep the pessimistic forces at bay.

• Sleep, or a lack of it, could be one of your problems now. When you do manage to sleep, you are likely to have nightmares. One of the ways you can stave off these nightmares each night as you prepare for sleep is to visualize yourself safe in the arms of an angel or in the embrace of the one who loves you. Keeping a dream journal can also help you to make sense of bad memories and anxieties. Ask your dream how to deal with your problem, and your question will be answered.

Secret: It is likely that you are currently plagued by panic attacks or have difficulty sleeping. This can be a serious drawback and may require medical or psychological attention. Don't berate yourself for those fears, but find healthy and preventative ways to handle them.

REVERSED

Quick Read: ***Deal with it.***

• You must learn to handle obsessive fears and compulsions; otherwise, they will consume and undermine your best interests. While you understand that at times your dark side intrudes on your waking life, you probably fear and distrust its influence. In darkness, your personal demons are sure to loom bigger and more menacing than ever, so you can expect your dream life to be somewhat difficult and unsettling at this time.

• You can lick this problem, but only if you are willing to confront it. Do not isolate yourself from the people you love, because their caring advice can help you to see past the darkness of the present and into the light that is your future. If you are desperate to begin a new relationship, you shouldn't allow your own unreasonable skepticism to interfere with your needs. You should also keep in mind that a lover is not meant to be a savior.

Secret: You find yourself reliving some of your childhood wounds. While you shouldn't feel shame about this, it may be necessary to seek treatment for those ghosts of the past. If you do not, you may continue to feel vulnerable and afraid. It's time to get in touch with your shadow side.

Ten of Swords

KEYWORDS

- Ruin • Betrayal
- Wounds • Therapy
- Dilemma • Failure

UPRIGHT

Quick Read: ***Have faith.***

• It is a difficult time for you, but even though the hopes and dreams of the past may have been dashed by a recent misfortune or loss, it is good to know that the worst is over. If you and a mate or dear friend are going through a tough time together, there is a chance that the current struggles could actually make your relationship stronger and more meaningful. Often, troubles faced together can produce greater wisdom and compassion between people.

• Your wounds are deep and it may take time for you to heal, but from the ashes of destroyed dreams will arise new dreams, new goals. This is one of those times when you need to "let go and let God." There is actually a great deal of liberation to be found in accepting the fact that you've lived through upheaval. You may have a lot more strength and ability to persevere than you thought.

Secret: Because of your distress, it may seem that you have little, if anything, to live for or to give to others at this time. The answer to these feelings is realizing that you are actually far luckier than many other people. Keep that in mind. Sharing and articulating your pain can help to comfort you.

REVERSED

Quick Read: ***Seek help for your problems.***

• You may feel that you are walking hand in hand with depression. The Ten of Swords reversed can signify that your recent sadness is almost too heavy to bear at this time. If romance is part of the problem, the tears you shed may convince you that true love will never be yours again. While the ending of a relationship can be devastating, you are only making things worse if you wallow in thoughts of misery and unhappiness.

• The remorse and anguish that you are experiencing now will pass in time, even if it feels as if they won't. You would be wise to seek out the help and support of friends or associates who have been through a similar travail. Dealing with a sense of hopelessness or having been abandoned requires a period of deep spiritual soul-searching before you are ready to rejoin the world once again.

Secret: You have been through a very heavy time. Don't shy away from seeking out professional help to get you through this unhappiness if that is what you need now. There is no shame in letting a specialist help you to heal. Isolating yourself will only make it hurt more.

Princess (or Page) of Swords

KEYWORDS

• Ideas • Theories
• Gossip • Surprises
• Communication
• Cleverness

UPRIGHT

Quick Read: ***Keep communicating.***

• The appearance of the Princess (or Page) of Swords in a reading often coincides with interesting news coming your way—good news that is likely to surprise you. Let others see that you have a talent for coming up with as well as implementing exciting new ideas. When you present yourself as a good communicator, you automatically get the respect you deserve.

• You are surrounded by a current of data, ideas, theories, and other bits and pieces of an overall plan that may take some figuring out. Abstract thinking will help you interpret a system or identify weak spots. This is a great time to gather information or seek out knowledge via books, magazines, the Internet, or even travel. Collecting essential details has the power to change your life. If you work in a communications-based field, you could be on the brink of a fantastically successful breakthrough.

Secret: You are full of clever ideas now! Don't be too clever for your own good, though. Information should be safeguarded. Keep new theories to yourself. Write them down. Don't be tempted to gossip, even favorably. Get ready for a good surprise!

REVERSED

Quick Read: ***Don't volunteer information!***

• If you are an unfocused person or a naive idealist, chances are you give away too much information and in general talk too much. The Princess (or Page) of Swords in reversed position usually indicates the presence of an immature or innocent person in your life. If this doesn't represent you, then it is likely to signify an individual who occupies an important place in your life. Avoid getting too involved with somebody new who fits this description.

• Communicating in a careless, slipshod way shows your inexperience. While you might enjoy indulging your eccentric side, this is not a good way to get others to respect you or your judgment. Your inability to be clear, concise, and well informed is sure to come back to haunt you. Where dating or romance is concerned, you need to guard against appearing to be too flirtatious, especially if your motives come across as insincere. Sending out the wrong signals could cause resentment if a person who really cares for you interprets them in the wrong way.

Secret: You must not leave your actions or words open to question at this time. A scandal could turn out to be your undoing if you aren't careful. Gossip could backfire. Privacy and discretion are important virtues for you now, but don't lie.

Prince (or Knight) of Swords

KEYWORDS

- Ingenuity • Domination
- Cunning • Defensiveness
- Aggression
- Outspokenness

UPRIGHT

Quick Read: ***Develop your ingenuity.***

• It is the perfect time to turn your daydreams into firm realities. Promote your self-esteem by speaking your mind intensely, as well as by engaging others in a battle of wits. This shows you have something to offer. You aren't afraid to fight for an idea, though you should guard against being too self-confident or appearing to be a know-it-all.

• You may have the opportunity to act in the role of teacher or mentor to a younger, less-experienced individual. As a matter of fact, you could find yourself magnetically drawn to an individual because of his or her intellect and openness. If there is an opportunity to get behind a cause that is dear to your heart, you can be expected to draw other people to your banner. Dreams have the opportunity to become solid reality now. Try to be more reflective and studious and you can reach your goals.

Secret: It is possible for you to express yourself forcefully without being argumentative or sarcastic. Learning to choose your words and attitude with care can save you from conflict with friends and associates. Don't be defensive.

REVERSED

Quick Read: ***Hold your tongue.***

• You can literally be your own worst enemy at this time, especially if you can't control your temper. In order to refute an opposing opinion, you may believe that you've got to prove the other person wrong in order to prove that you are right, but that isn't the case. True, you are willing to make big sacrifices for the compelling belief so dear to your heart, but if you aren't careful you will alienate rather than convince others with your aggressiveness.

• There is a great deal of flux going on in your life right now, and as a result you could be feeling anxious and defensive. Even though your plan of action is sure to be brave and brilliant, it may be totally impractical. An outspoken person who appears on the scene at this time could prove to be a powerful rival. You and a partner could be at odds over a subject, and although you enjoy a good fight, beware of destructive attitudes that can hurt the relationship.

Secret: A work colleague could be itching to pull you into a controversy. Either you are the clever, cunning, and outspoken person or you will find yourself dealing with an individual who fits that description. Think a bit before you blurt out words that you might regret.

Queen of Swords

KEYWORDS
• *Independence*
• *Truthfulness* • *Bitterness*
• *Self-sufficiency* • *Difficulty*
• *Prudishness*

UPRIGHT

Quick Read: ***Speak your truth.***

• You are a strong and independent soul, and that is the apex of your personal power. You should use your ideas and insight to establish your power and stoke the success that you have worked for and deserve. Unfortunately, that is easier said than done, particularly if emotions are in play.

• Because of a current situation that necessitates that you be serious and firm, empathy toward others is not advised. This is not a time for being weak or sentimental.

• Use information in a straightforward, analytical way and as a means to achieve necessary changes. Come out and tell it like it is. Assert your right to go from frightening to frivolous as well as anywhere in between! You may not have all the answers, but you have most of them. If you don't have the level of independence you want, do whatever is needed in order to accomplish this change in circumstances.

Secret: Power and knowledge can be a burden. The sheer volume of information and reasoning you must deal with now requires you to be very direct and efficient. It can enrich your life if you know how to use your influence without letting emotions get in the way.

REVERSED

Quick Read: ***Be strong, but not too strong!***

• At this time, an inability to assert your independence will block your progress. If you can't function well on your own, you will waste time. If you are not the individual who fits the Queen of Swords' esoteric description, it could be that someone very much like her is blocking you from accomplishing the total independence you have been seeking.

• If a relationship is a part of your focus at this time, you need to make sure you are involved for all the right reasons. You might be afraid of getting involved, fearful that by giving your heart you will give up the independence you so greatly prize. You should avoid getting serious about a partner who doesn't share your need for intellectual stimulation. Another problematic relationship can be where either one or both of you are trying to work on the other for the other's good.

Secret: If you are lonely, be careful that it doesn't turn your strength into rigidity and prudishness. If you are feeling unloved, it is easy to mask your feelings with coldness, but that will be a hindrance rather than a help.

King of Swords

KEYWORDS
- Intellect • Authority
- Rules • Brainstorm
- Diplomacy • Forcefulness

UPRIGHT

Quick Read: ***Tap into your mind power.***

• The realm of ideas is familiar territory for you. Your schooling and knowledge of philosophy are important, but don't discount your idle thoughts and daydreams. They can also be instrumental in helping you solve problems and make decisions. Diplomacy, a sense of history, and the ability to know what is best suggest the premier qualities of the King of Swords. If this doesn't describe you, it could represent someone who has recently entered your life.

• Because of your intellectual bent, you are able to stay calm, focused, and fair yet be forceful when other people become overly emotional and scattered. You can also use your high-minded ideas to plot a course for the future. People will listen to your brainstorms. Rules and laws have special significance at this time, and you should abide by them. Rationality goes only so far, though, so don't completely rule out being influenced by your heart as well as your intellect.

Secret: Valuing the force of your intellect or that of someone close to you is important now. Visualize yourself on a cloud gazing down, watching the history of the world playing out beneath you. The power of ideas has shaped the world. Appreciate and use them to your advantage.

REVERSED

Quick Read: ***Living in your head weakens you.***

• Intellect, reason, and analysis are wonderful traits, but at the present time they can get in the way of common sense. Intellect can be at odds with wisdom in both your professional and your private life. It can also block your progress now, especially if your theories are unworkable when they are put into practice. Dealing on a strictly intellectual level can be a mistake if you are trying to forge a close and intimate relationship. Although you believe in being fair and impartial, you could find that your judgment is somewhat impaired by preconceived ideas at this time.

• If you are currently dealing with an austere, authoritarian individual, you might find it hard to get your own ideas across. If this man is a boss, you may fear that you won't be promoted. If he is a mate or partner, it could be hard for you to create a sense of equality in your relationship.

Secret: You should beware of behaving in a way that causes associates to see you as a snob. Your cool, rational mind is one of your finest features, but you shouldn't use it as a barrier between yourself and other people. Try to be more diplomatic, not so judgmental.

CUPS

(also known as Water, Hearts, Chalices, or Shells)

Ace of Cups

KEYWORDS

- *Magnetism* • *New love*
- *Compassion* • *Desires*
- *Poignancy* • *Open heart*

UPRIGHT

Quick Read: ***Be open to love.***

• This is a time in your life when you are surrounded by immense happiness and creative energy. The Ace of Cups always signifies a wonderful new beginning—a period when you are eager to initiate a new project that you will truly love. Being new isn't enough to make it special—let this be something that both excites and challenges you. That way you will be motivated to follow your passion.

• Opening your heart to a new romance can be a fabulous experience now. Don't be surprised if true love is given and received in equal measure. If you are already in a relationship, the union will blossom anew, and you will know the deepening of a mutual commitment. Be spontaneous, creative, and open to all things. Nothing can hold you back now, so long as you break through all illusions.

Secret: Joy, health, happiness, and excitement are being offered to you on the proverbial silver platter. Don't ignore these gifts of love or allow them to go unappreciated. Allow yourself to feel the positive benefits flowing into and out of your heart.

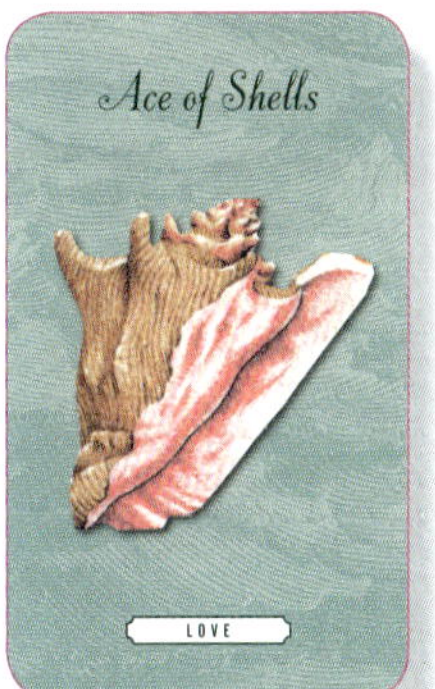

REVERSED

Quick Read: ***Learn to trust your heart.***

• Even though you may feel ready to take on a new project, in some distant corner of your mind there could be a nagging voice that second-guesses your choice and questions your ability to follow through. Alternatively, you may lack the energy and initiative that it takes in order to begin a new project.

• If the new project is an attempt at a new romance, you may be afraid to make the first move beyond simply falling in love. At the beginning of a new love affair, everything is enhanced by the transcendent nature of romance. However, the fear of commitment in you or the person you love could be a barrier that leaves you feeling vaguely unfulfilled. Once you learn to move beyond your defenses, you will realize that these are feelings that money can't buy and time cannot take away from you.

Secret: In the past, you may have been treated thoughtlessly by a parent, lover, or mate, though this poor treatment may have been unintentional. This has left a poignant mark, making it hard for you to trust. Learn to heal this old wound by opening your heart and allowing a new love energy to enter.

Two of Cups

KEYWORDS

- *Romance* • *Equality*
- *Support* • *Laughter*
- *Affection* • *Tenderness*

UPRIGHT

Quick Read: ***The Law of Attraction works wonders.***

• The Two of Cups signifies that this is a wonderful and loving time for you. Whether the relationship in question is romantic, familial, or business related, there is a supportive and nurturing exchange between you and another person. At this time, you need to present yourself as a rare and lucky person who has the chance to be one-half of a loving, vibrant, and supportive couple—whether romantic or otherwise. If you are alone and looking for someone to share your life with, it is time to turn on your "love light."

• Where romance is concerned, there is a definite potential for a loving union to develop and for passion to grow. There is a chance that in the days and weeks to come there will be a heartfelt emotional exchange of some sort between the two of you, though it is possible that more will be revealed later.

Secret: If you are not romantically involved with someone now but want to be, put your yearnings to good use by visualizing how your ideal partner will be. Feel how you will feel when the two of you are together. This is known as the Law of Attraction and acts as a magnet to attract what you visualize.

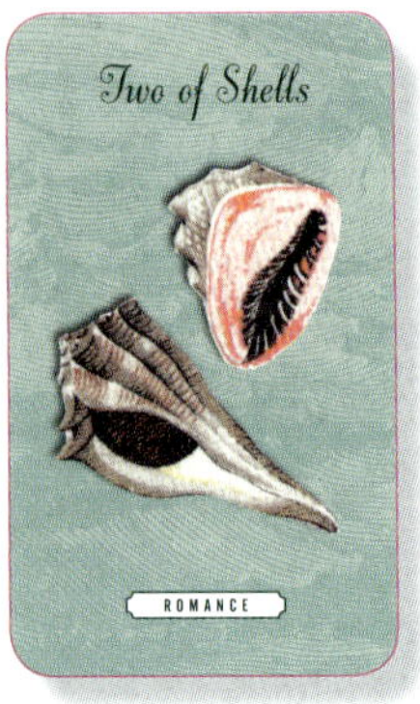

REVERSED

Quick Read: ***Love requires cooperation and thoughtfulness.***

• Even if a loving relationship seems to have come your way, you probably feel unsure about the relationship, questioning your ability to commit or worrying about what is ahead for the two of you. Alternatively, you might think that over time, your deepest and most profound feelings will not be reciprocated.

• One of the reasons you may be having a problem drawing love into your life is a subconscious fear that in order to embrace true love you will have to give up a measure of your own independence. Perhaps you find yourself attracted to someone but are unsure of how that individual feels about you. It is possible that a romantic partner is causing a problem in your life right now, and you might feel as if you are being held back as a result. In any relationship—romantic, business, or family—an individual can bloom only if both parties have an equal voice.

Secret: You should not allow yourself to fall in love with love, even if it is tempting to do so. Losing yourself in a romantic relationship can be as bad as having no love life at all. There is a chance that the relationship will end up being unbalanced, unfair, or one-sided.

Three of Cups

KEYWORDS

• Celebration • Fun • Gratitude • Charity • Hospitality

UPRIGHT

Quick Read: ***It's party time!***

• There is a festive atmosphere, you are filled with gratitude for all of life's wonderful gifts, and you aren't in the least bit shy about letting others know how you feel. Be a living example of the power of faith, hope, and charity without appearing to take these things for granted. The art of sharing will help you in everything you do.

• Currently, you are supported by loving, caring friends who are inspired by your exuberance and joie de vivre. In return, their spirit will infuse yours with a sense of the best that life has to offer. Put your worries aside and experience a true sense of joy and fulfillment. Speak your heart unapologetically about who and what are most important to you. Visualize yourself becoming richer by expressing gratitude to those you love. This is the time to throw the sort of party you've always wanted to attend!

Secret: This is a time when you will want to celebrate your good fortune with the people you love. Whether through money, friendship, or acts of kindness, you know how to spread the good cheer around equally. Attend or host a special social gathering.

REVERSED

Quick Read: ***Keep it simple.***

• Court moderation at this time, or it is likely that you will have very little to celebrate. Because you might feel as if things are generally going your way now, it can be hard for you to rein in your enthusiasm for living life in an extravagant way. You need to face up to the fact that splurging on too much of anything—food, drink, money, fun—can be a big mistake.

• It is possible that your plans for a vacation or celebration cannot be realized at this time. There is also a chance that you and a lover or mate could discover that once the party is over, the two of you aren't compatible. If you are having trouble finding things to celebrate, it is time to make up some reasons to do so. Write "Celebrate" at the top of a piece of paper and make a to-do list underneath it. It is a good exercise to feel grateful for all the true riches in your life.

Secret: Shy away from a "party person" during this period, since this individual is likely to be a superficial friend at best. He or she may bring out the shallow side of your nature or tempt you to fritter away your time. It is good to be moderate now—go the middle way.

Four of Cups

KEYWORDS
• Reevaluation • Waste
• Insight • Dissatisfaction
• Complaints • Regret

UPRIGHT

Quick Read: ***Don't cry over spilled milk.***

• If you are feeling bored, confused, or disillusioned about where your life is going, it may be time to make some well-considered changes. Taking time for a period of introspection can help revitalize your spirit as well as your point of view.

• It doesn't do any good to be unhappy about something that has already happened. Whatever mistakes were made—by you or someone close to you—leave them in the past. It is time to review, accept the truth, and then move forward once again. If you are the person who is being reevaluated, do not stress about the outcome. The opinion of others is important, but most important of all is how you see and value yourself. While you may have complaints and dissatisfaction, you need to move beyond these distractions, or you will become a victim of your regret.

Secret: You fear that an old friend or a family member may say "I told you so" regarding a recent failure, undercutting your confidence and self-esteem. It is a waste of time to fret over perceived mistakes.

REVERSED

Quick Read: ***Reexamine your goals.***

• A period of emotional introspection and quiet is just what you need if you want to change your future. Keep in mind that you shouldn't reenter the world of social activities until you have reexamined your personal value system. It is always tempting to postpone this process, but all that does is postpone the eventual pain of this situation. Take some time to think, but don't fixate on circumstances that cannot be helped.

• Where a relationship is concerned, the two of you need to be on the same page. Recently, emotions have changed, and whether that is for good or for ill, those changes need to be acknowledged and acted upon. If you are looking for a healthy partnership, you need to reevaluate your own ability to commit. Don't ignore it, but don't obsess over it, either. Offering each other insights and setting new goals as partners will help to soothe cranky or stress-producing communications.

Secret: Beware of the instability that comes from constantly questioning yourself and your ideas. Decide where you have gone astray and what must change as a result, then be done with it. Stand by your decision. Learn from your mistakes.

Five of Cups

KEYWORDS
• Disappointment
• Rejection • Insecurity
• Depression • Setbacks
• Letting go

UPRIGHT

Quick Read: ***Is the glass half full or half empty?***

• Even though this may be a time of disenchantment, there is a chance for you to turn things around, depending on your attitude. For example, try looking at the glass as half full instead of half empty! Yes, there may be problems—even roadblocks—to your happiness and success right now, but with the proper attitude you can work through them. Accept disappointments, even the fact that you might have to walk away from someone or something that means a lot to you.

• It is important to realize and understand that disillusionment is a part of life, but it doesn't have to keep you from finding happiness and satisfaction in the future. Disappointment and rejection can even provide useful experience of a sort. You can learn from this and actually grow stronger. At all costs, avoid self-medicating if you feel depressed or despondent.

Secret: Fear of failure can be a paralyzing problem, keeping you from taking chances that could improve your lot in life. If that is the case, seek professional help in order to move beyond feelings of rejection and loneliness. Work on letting go of and looking beyond disappointment.

REVERSED

Quick Read: ***Don't be in denial.***

• Sometimes it is hard—even impossible—to enjoy the happiness of the present because of issues and emotional encumbrances from the past. Every period of life has its drawbacks and sadness, but the problems of today are sufficient without mulling over those of the past. If you have a hard time separating today's challenges from those of another time, you may need the help of a skilled professional to put things into perspective.

• The worst thing you can do is let an old problem impose on the present. No relationship, regardless of how much love there is, can withstand that sort of pressure. Problems that are not severe should be dealt with in the present relationship, or they will come back again in a different form or a different relationship. Naturally, if you are involved in a union where there is violence or some other form of abuse, it is time to walk away

Secret: Denial never helps anyone. If you are currently denying that you're experiencing disappointment in love or another relationship, you are fooling yourself, and even that won't last for long. Face up to your pain and it will pass. Don't be afraid to seek help.

Six of Cups

KEYWORDS

• Joy • Remembrance
• Nostalgia • Innocence
• Childhood • Pleasure

UPRIGHT

Quick Read: ***It's time to lighten up!***

• This is a delightful and cheerful influence. Childlike joy will soon be yours. It is likely that you will be reminded of a happy childhood memory. A fond sense of nostalgia might be easily triggered because of a short trip you make or a gift given to you by a friend or a loved one. Try to become more aware of the fact that these feelings are always there for you. All they need is to be gathered up and appreciated, like a bouquet of sweet-scented flowers.

• Do yourself a favor and make ample time for yourself. By being as open, trusting, and optimistic as a child, you open yourself up to new ideas and pleasant influences. Surround yourself with young people and tap into their energy. Savor past memories, experiencing them with all your senses. You will have a renewed appreciation for family life and especially a little child, either your own or someone else's.

Secret: You can benefit from spending time with younger people, even very young children. Their innocence can be a reminder to you that cynicism and negative thoughts are the refuge of the lonely and the bitter. Take pleasure in fond recollections.

REVERSED

Quick Read: ***Don't be childish; be childlike.***

• Someone or something from your past may be troubling you at this time, creating a sense of tension and even fear. You or somebody that you love very much may have anxiety about what lies ahead, causing you to find solace in the past, or at least in memories of what you choose to see as a happier time.

• At times it can be tempting to look back at your childhood or youth and feel as if you were happier then. You could be obsessed with the good old days, believing that you can't enjoy yourself now as you did at that time. Alternatively, you might call up unpleasant memories from your childhood and feel resentful that you cannot seem to move beyond them. You may fear painful memories of a paradise lost, or you might be anxious about having responsibility for a young child.

Secret: You have been squelching the child that dwells within, who needs love and fun and playfulness. Perhaps you have become jaded or believe that others will think less of you if you show this side of your nature, but you are wrong.

Seven of Cups

KEYWORDS

• *Illusion* • *Wishes*
• *Escapism* • *Fantasy*
• *Vacillation*
• *Misconception*

UPRIGHT

Quick Read: ***Do not delude yourself.***

• At the present time, you are surrounded by a great many choices, as well as the confusion of discerning what is real and what is an illusion. While it is wonderful to have many alternatives at one time, it can also cause a great deal of uncertainty and perplexity. Your idealism is sweeping you away to the point where it can be hard to keep a grip on reality. There may also be a chance of mood swings relating to your current romantic situation.

• This doesn't mean that wishes can't come true. See a picture of yourself, of your life, in your mind's eye, and visualize your wish becoming a reality. There is glamour, almost intoxication, in the dreamlike world of fantasy, which can be extremely provocative. Just try to keep from letting the fantasy overwhelm your common sense.

Secret: There is a possibility that your idealization of an individual or an idea has blinded you to the faults of this person or the pitfalls that your fantasy may actually have. Rather than deceiving yourself, be willing to see the truth. Know that you have alternatives.

REVERSED

Quick Read: ***Don't think with your heart.***

• When the Seven of Cups is reversed, you may find it very hard to distinguish creative impulses from mere pipedreams. Wishful thinking is likely to take over now, especially if you fear taking decisive action. You or someone close to you could be deliberately or subconsciously misinterpreting ideas or information. For this reason, it is best to hold off making important choices now, or you might end up opting for decisions that are impractical, to say the least.

• Because of your desire for escapism, you may find it hard to focus on reality now. All efforts might feel like work. When it comes to matters of the heart, you could find yourself drawn into an unwise and ultimately unworkable relationship. The problem is that even though you may think you love this person with all of your heart, he or she might not believe you or return your love.

Secret: Illusion can be a barrier to progress and happiness at this point in your life. There is a difference between being open to fantasy and living in a fantasy world. Avoid being too distracted to acknowledge the truth of your situation. Don't make a big decision at this time.

Eight of Cups

KEYWORDS
• Sacrifice • Insincerity
• Weariness • Demoralized
• Downtrodden
• Resentment

UPRIGHT

Quick Read: ***Make your boundaries.***

• You need to create some boundaries in your life—not to keep others out but for purposes of demarcation. There must be a retreat now from emotional involvement. You are weary of giving away too much of yourself; you have been left feeling drained, discouraged, and resentful. Now you need to heal. Past sacrifices affect your present situation, and whether you realize it or not, you are beginning to resent the time and effort you have spent on others to the detriment of your own happiness and fulfillment.

• You must become more aware of the physical, mental, or emotional sacrifices required by a particular situation. If you determine that it is all too much for you, then you may have to seek out a person or cause that is more worthy of your efforts. To underpin your efforts, vow to be less shy. Don't take yourself so seriously, either.

Secret: You are finally learning how to give yourself the care and emotional nurturing that you have neglected for such a long time. At last you have the opportunity and the motivation to improve your well-being and not be so drained by others.

REVERSED

Quick Read: ***Don't be too self-sacrificing.***

• This can be a precarious period for you, filled with self-doubt and pessimistic thoughts. It may even feel as if you are being drained of everything you hold dear. You might wonder why you are feeling so angry and neglected, especially when you are doing the right thing by being the selfless one in your marriage or other relationship.

• The real problem is that after a while, even a dream relationship can turn into a nightmare if there is an imbalance of sacrifice. Ask yourself if this is related to a lowered level of self-esteem in your past. If you are continuing to give far more than you are getting in return, it is time that you find someone who values you more than your current partner. This influence may suggest that you are not yet ready for a relationship in which you are an equal partner. Professional therapy may be required.

Secret: Don't be a martyr to love in your relationship. A true union requires sacrifice from both partners, not just you. You shouldn't give so much to your partner that you have nothing left to nourish your own needs and goals. Your pessimism needs to be addressed.

Nine of Cups

KEYWORDS

- *Fulfillment* • *Realization* • *Wish* • *Happiness* • *Satisfaction* • *Gifts*

UPRIGHT

Quick Read: ***Your wish is granted!***

• In any reading, the Nine of Cups has great magical significance. Not only will a current wish come true, but also more than likely it will be granted in a happy way. Now is the time for all the wonderful gifts you have been yearning for to come your way—good health, success in material and esoteric matters, and an awesome relationship. If fulfillment of your wishes for these good things has been delayed, you will find even more satisfaction in their realization at this time.

• Remember that when formulating a specific wish, you should be sure to phrase it as precisely as you possibly can. You should be open to the fact that the wish might be granted in an unexpected, even surprising way. It might not be immediately obvious just how this matter improves your life, but you will discover it—and be glad of it—in due time.

Secret: Be constantly aware of the good luck you are enjoying during this time. It is a blessed respite that can give you a sense of satisfaction and pleasure at a future time when things may not be so pleasant. Enjoy your wish!

REVERSED

Quick Read: ***Be careful what you wish for.***

• People don't always know what fork in the road they should take. Sometimes we need to take a broader view of things. What is certain is that there is some form of fulfillment waiting in the wings. It is important for you to remember that a wish or goal that is very close to your heart may not be in your best interests. At times you might not be able to see how lucky you are, especially if you believe that your current circumstances are at odds with your wish.

• If you are feeling conflicted, wondering whether your true wish will materialize, you need to turn your reasoning upside down and take a look at how many times in the past your wishes have come true. This can be a very difficult time if you are accustomed to getting your way. Learn to trust in the universe and what it provides.

Secret: You should not be narrow-minded in the way that you expect your wish to come true. We don't always know exactly what is best for us. If there is a different destiny meant for you, that is what will happen. There are hidden, unused gifts that you may be overlooking.

Ten of Cups

KEYWORDS

• *Accomplishment* • *Bliss* • *Success* • *Kindness* • *Contentment* • *Respect*

UPRIGHT

Quick Read: *Success will be yours!*

• There are many types of success, and drawing the Ten of Cups suggests that you are on the brink of great domestic happiness, maybe even a marriage, and personal success. Visualize the many goals you have attained, and consider the many people who would be thrilled to have what you have at this point in time. However, keep in mind that you will not totally enjoy your success unless you empower yourself by truly appreciating what you have done. This card also signifies a time of contentment and peace in all your important personal relationships.

• As in the past when you were successful, you will be respected for your efforts. Additionally, successful dealings will bring you an overwhelming amount of honor from friends and peers. In order to avoid the negative effects of the envy of those who might be jealous of what you have accomplished, show yourself to be kind, gracious, and humble.

Secret: You should look to the advice of an accomplished person who may be able to help you attain a much-desired goal. This individual may be destined to become a part of your spiritual family. Give yourself credit for your achievements—you deserve your success.

REVERSED

Quick Read: *Fear of failure can paralyze your actions.*

• This is no time for nitpicking. Perhaps despite the fact that things are going well for you now, you might find it hard to believe that your success will last. A habit of being pessimistic could keep you from having the motivation to reach your goals. You might be tempted to focus on a failure from your past, creating feelings of inadequacy. However, too much glorying in past triumphs can make you seem opinionated and arrogant.

• Someone you love or care about may not be feeling successful at this time, and it might be up to you to help change that attitude. There are people who love you who may nonetheless get in the way of your success. Don't let this happen. Even if your current family situation is complicated by frustrating and dysfunctional relationships, don't concentrate all of your energy on trying to be a fixer at the risk of ignoring your personal goals.

Secret: Your worry may be that the price of success is too high, and because of it you are unsure of how diligently you should work to achieve a goal. This attitude can keep you from becoming what you want. Being a perfectionist can inhibit you.

Princess (or Page) of Cups

KEYWORDS

• Fondness • Affection
• Tenderness • Intuition
• Dreams • Sensitivity

UPRIGHT

Quick Read: ***Communicate your feelings.***

• The presence of the Princess of Cups in a reading signifies emotional tendencies and a sensitive spirit. Soon you may meet, or find yourself behaving like, an engaging young person whose head rules his or her heart. Fantasies can go just so far, however, and it is important that you balance your creativity and emotional responses with logic and the desire to see things the way they really are.

• You may feel inexperienced, even timid, and not ready for the responsibilities that come with a serious relationship. Despite this fear, you need to try. At this time, you have to concentrate on the communication of your most tender feelings, hunches, and dreams. If you are unable to do this, you may not be able to make a wonderful new relationship work in your favor. Expect to learn an amazing amount about communicating your psychic intuitiveness to others.

Secret: Your current situation is not unlike being pregnant—you need to give birth to tender feelings, bringing them into a loving world where they are prized, needed, and wanted. You are their "mother" and will continue to tend them. Listen to your dreams. Be gentle.

REVERSED

Quick Read: ***Your foolish heart may trick you.***

• Your idealism is unlikely to be rewarded now, especially if you are indolent and emotionally needy. It is possible that you don't have the emotional experience or maturity to sustain a romantic relationship, even though it means a great deal to you. Although you have many tender feelings, especially about a loved one, you might not have the courage to communicate those feelings or put them on display.

• More than likely, you have all of the intuitiveness in your nature that is suggested by this card. Unfortunately, you don't know what to do with it. You are full of fears now—afraid that you might give away your heart too easily. You may be in denial when it comes to emotional conflicts, being a sucker for any hard-luck story someone feeds you. It is difficult for you to handle all of the feelings, emotions, and hunches coming at you now without feeling totally overwhelmed and weakened by them.

Secret: You are too emotionally naive to make the best of a new relationship. Your feelings may have been hurt. It would help to date casually—don't give away your heart too freely. The possibility of pregnancy or metaphorical birth is an issue that needs to be addressed with care.

Prince (or Knight) of Cups

KEYWORDS

• Charm • Poetry
• Secrets • Exploration
• Flirtation • Sexuality

UPRIGHT

Quick Read: ***Try a poetic view of life.***

• Currently, it is vital that you show the charming, romantic side of your nature. Don't be afraid to do a little innocent flirting, especially if you have been in a serious phase of life recently. In the past, being charming and attractive to others (regardless of their sex) and expressing the romantic, poetic view of life has gotten you what you need.

• If you do not typify the characteristics of the Prince of Cups, it is highly likely that you will soon meet someone who does. This individual could turn out to be a love interest, or perhaps he or she will inspire you, even introduce you to an exceptional and creative new circle of friends. It is even likely that, as a result of these new interests, you will attract invitations and some new contacts. Whomever you meet and whatever you do, now is the time to explore feelings of young love.

Secret: Keep romance alive in your life. Visualize yourself in a love scene from one of your favorite movies. Savor your feelings—feel every one that you can. Stay in touch with your "true love spirit," explore your sexuality, and remember to keep secrets to yourself.

REVERSED

Quick Read: ***Don't lose your way.***

• It is easy to lose your bearings now, particularly if you are too much in the company of a goalless, hedonistic type of individual. The charms of this person may be little more than a facade, and by spending time with him or her, you are allowing your own will and energy to be thwarted. If sex or romance is involved in the relationship, you could find yourself giving in to the emotional demands of someone who really isn't good for you. You should not believe all you hear at this time because there are sure to be lies aimed at getting you into trouble.

• The Prince of Cups reversed can reflect addictive traits such as drinking, drugs, or sexual promiscuity. If you have a proclivity to such behavior, you could discover that the need for more intense pleasures might deteriorate into little more than empty promises.

Secret: If you are shy, you may be afraid to explore your sexuality at this time. Ask yourself if you are uncomfortable with the superficial or if it's something deeper, like an inability to invite intimacy, either physical or emotional. You may feel lost or lonely now. Beware of addictions.

Queen of Cups

KEYWORDS

• *Empathy* • *Nurturing*
• *Caring* • *Clairvoyance*
• *Meddling* • *Devotion*

UPRIGHT

Quick Read: ***Show you care.***

• It is time for you to be sensitive to human frailties, including your own. Even though it might be somewhat painful to deal with your emotions, you can learn how to channel them in order to help those who are weighed down by life's challenges. Being kind, compassionate, and caring puts you on a truly spiritual path.

• Articulating your deepest feelings in an honest way can be hard, especially if you are afraid that your words may hurt someone you care about. Your psychic abilities can be very much in evidence now, allowing you to decipher how to solve problems. Alternatively, you may seek to align yourself with an empathic, sensitive individual who seems to understand you even better than you understand yourself. A sensitive and intuitive dreamer has the amazing power to teach you a great deal about affection, devotion, faith, and even forgiveness.

Secret: Be a shoulder for a close friend to cry on, but respect your friend's boundaries, too. Being able to help others means giving them a hand, not a handout. Don't be codependent. Learn how to listen.

REVERSED

Quick Read: ***Don't absorb the negativity of others.***

• This card reversed suggests just how important it is that you adopt a harder shell in order to shield yourself from those who might take advantage of your compassionate nature. Your intuition is divinely inspired, but it must be used to empower and not enable others. Helping them to become more emotionally independent can be your crowning achievement. Are you the person who has the unfocused, even confused ways of the Queen of Cups? If that doesn't describe you, it is possible that you will soon meet an individual who has these characteristics.

• Be sure to guard against codependent or enabling behavior, either in yourself or in someone close to you. If it is a person you love, visualize yourself actively living their life from their point of view. If you are enabling a lover or mate, their bad habits or neediness could eventually become a burden or even cause you heartbreak. You must let them learn their own lessons.

Secret: Don't be tempted to play the victim, even if you are feeling somewhat vulnerable at this point in your life. Don't take on everyone else's problems. If you have the need to talk things out, seek out a good friend or even a professional therapist.

King of Cups

KEYWORDS

• Consideration • Healer • Counselor • Jealousy • Understanding • Artist

UPRIGHT

Quick Read: *Master your emotions.*

• It is vital that you make a concentrated effort to be very understanding at this time, especially since you may be called upon to counsel others. This is a time when you need to look deep within yourself in order to learn what gifts you have to offer as a lover, parent, mate, counselor, and friend. You should not be intimidated by the fact that others see you as a leader. Remember to give advice only to those who ask you for it and who you know are ready to receive it.

• Now it is important that you view your life as a work of art and your art as a work of life, because they are inseparable. This is not the time to repress your honest emotions. You have strong feelings that have surfaced recently, and you need to examine and appreciate them.

Secret: You are able to help others by being considerate, kind, and understanding. You have a big heart or may meet someone with that healing characteristic. There is a chance that others may be jealous. You also may have artistic inspirations and talents, so use your gifts.

REVERSED

Quick Read: *Beware of addictive behavior.*

• You or someone close to you has many gifts, many talents, but they are worthless if they are lorded over people who may not be lucky enough to possess them. Remember that creativity and an appreciation for the arts are things to be prized, not paraded. As soon as you begin to think of yourself as superior to the people around you, you have taken a small step toward losing your humanity.

• You could find yourself drawn to other people's problems, but overreacting emotionally instead of responding rationally won't help either of you. If you have a psychic realization regarding someone you love or even a person you work with, it could be a burden. If these traits or proclivities do not define or explain your own behavior, you could soon find yourself acting in concert with an individual who has many of the affecting characteristics embodied by the King of Cups. Be conscious of tendencies of escapism and addictions.

Secret: Forgiveness is a key factor in all relationships. Don't allow yourself to be stuck in the past. Just because you once had a strong antipathy toward someone doesn't mean that these negative feelings must remain. Forget them and move on. Beware of intoxications.

PENTACLES

(also known as Earth, Diamonds, Coins, or Gems)

Ace of Pentacles

KEYWORDS

• Enterprise • Reward
• Power • Wealth
• Opportunity • Potential

UPRIGHT

Quick Read: ***Reap your reward.***

• What a great time this is for you! The Ace of Pentacles is one of the most fortunate cards in the entire Tarot deck. Even if you don't realize it, you have worked for and earned the wonderful rewards and happiness that are coming your way. Very soon you shall have enough resources to do and possess whatever you want. Don't feel bad about presenting yourself as a prosperous individual. Show that you have a new opportunity for financial gain. You have the golden touch, so flaunt it!

• The chance for making money is very real now, and if you apply the lessons of this reading, you should be able to claim your rich reward. Visualize the law of cause and effect working to give you all that you deserve. Believe in the idea that consistent visualization practices produce wonderful results. You need to understand that your reward may come to you in an unexpected way.

Secret: The rewards you have been able to draw into your life are a fine example to others who may seek to achieve the same thing. Your ability to believe wholeheartedly in yourself is inspiring to those who look up to you. You deserve the riches you can now reap.

REVERSED

Quick Read: ***Don't give up.***

• There are times when more can be too much, and the Ace of Pentacles reversed suggests that this may be one of them. If you sit back and expect things to simply come to you, it is possible that you will lose out on a variety of wonderful blessings—the great job, the perfect relationship, the fabulous financial opportunity.

• Believe it or not, you could actually be afraid of success and good fortune. You might feel as if you don't deserve to prosper, or perhaps you secretly fear the additional responsibilities that come with having a lot of money. There is always the chance that if you have more cash on hand, people will expect more from you. By the same token, if you try to use wealth as a way to manipulate others, you will end up being the one who is manipulated.

Secret: Receiving a reward shouldn't be the main goal. If it is, you will not enjoy long-lived success. Don't feel as if you are entitled to something you cannot afford or feel you should have, and don't be bitter because a reward you think you deserve has been too long in coming.

Two of Pentacles

KEYWORDS

• *Change* • *Flexibility*
• *Instability* • *Multitasking*
• *Juggling* • *Balance*

UPRIGHT

Quick Read: ***Stay centered.***

• One of the biggest challenges in modern life is trying to juggle more than one task or one responsibility at a time. This card indicates that you will need to stay flexible while keeping informed about upcoming changes. You cannot expect things to stay the same for very long. During this period you might find yourself juggling more than one job or project, or you might have to focus on the best way to multitask in the areas of your relationships, career, and family.

• In the past, you have endured changes, both comfortable and uncomfortable, and now you are being called upon to do so again. It is vital that you look upon this edict for change as a profound opportunity instead of a burden. Visualize yourself within the eye of a hurricane, remaining calm and quiet no matter how fast the howling winds circle you.

Secret: This can be an unstable time, so keep hold of the ideas and values that mean something special to you now. While you need to be open to change, you also need to feel centered, both emotionally and spiritually. Learn how to switch gears when necessary.

REVERSED

Quick Read: ***Pick up the pieces.***

• You may feel that a big problem at this time is that you are being pulled in too many directions at once. Because of the stress of these extra demands, you may find it hard to keep everything from falling apart. Losing control of a situation is something you worry about now. It is also possible that a changeable or unstable person will cause some difficulty for you now.

• During this time you are likely to be tested by a great deal of change, busyness and tension. While this can be a strong motivation, it can also cause you to feel nervous and unfocused. You might not be sure just what is expected of you, or, if you do know, you may worry that you cannot possibly live up to the expectations that others have of you. You may be afraid that a tough or stressful situation will never fully resolve itself to your or someone else's best hopes.

Secret: Your current problems could be the result of somebody who is two-faced and manipulative or who is hiding his or her problems from you and from the world. Just make certain that you are not the guilty party!

Three of Pentacles

KEYWORDS

• Work • Production
• Artistry • Business
• Consideration
• Conscientiousness

UPRIGHT

Quick Read: ***Shared burdens are lighter.***

• Whatever work you do, visualize that work as caring for a garden. See yourself carefully preparing the soil, planting, weeding, and reaping the harvest. There is an old saying—"You reap what you sow." You cannot plant onions and expect to grow roses. You should also be aware that you aren't going to be working alone—there are people at your side who are willing, even anxious to help you.

• Remember that work shared is work halved. You will be able to depend on a friend, colleague, or co-worker. If you and a partner are working toward a goal together—whether a personal or professional aspiration—you need to pitch in to support and sustain each other. It is also an excellent time to seek the advice of a trusted friend or counselor, someone who is pleased to share techniques, solutions, and business aspirations.

Secret: One of life's great joys is doing work that is satisfying. This is the time to roll up your sleeves and realize the rewards of tasks thoroughly and well executed for their own sake. Be conscientious and allow others to help, and your efforts will produce fine results.

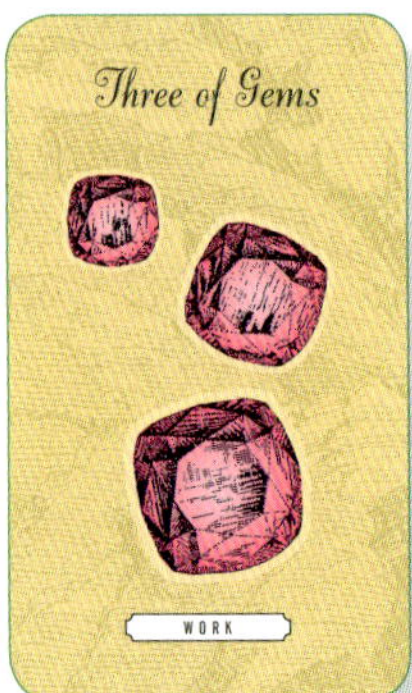

REVERSED

Quick Read: ***You are not easily satisfied.***

• The Three of Pentacles reversed can signify that you are currently unsatisfied with your lot in life but don't really know what to do about it. It is possible that you find yourself trapped in a dead-end job or, at the very least, uninspired by work that has become routine and boring. If you have lost the taste for work you used to love, you might be unsure of what you need to replace it. Having a defeatist attitude will only make things worse.

• The same can be true of a relationship that may have lost its fervor. If you are unattached, you may need to question the common sense of becoming romantically involved with a person you work with—whether it is a superior, a colleague, or someone who works for you. This is almost certain to be a mistake, born of the fact that you might be confusing a romantic dalliance for the work-related satisfaction you have been seeking.

Secret: You should understand that you don't need another person to complete who you are. Whether or not you have a wonderful partner, lover, mate, or friend, you are ultimately responsible for your own satisfaction, your own happiness. Try to change a boring routine.

Four of Pentacles

KEYWORDS

• Possessiveness • Conservation • Greed • Management • Purchases • Transactions

UPRIGHT

Quick Read: ***Hold on to what you have.***

• Your main concern now is to hang on to what you have rather than bargain for something new. Reflect on the quality of your own values and self-worth. These are highly prized, precious virtues that cannot be taken away from you, only given away. Whether these matters involve money, your professional reputation, or a relationship, show that your priorities are in order and that you can manage and protect all that you are responsible for.

• Most important of all, you need to be aware that true security comes from within. Material gains alone will not satisfy your need for security. Also, if you do not wish to appear greedy, you should let others see that your motivation is not based solely on how much money you can make. Be conservative, but don't close yourself off from fresh and equally important opportunities.

Secret: At this time you could find yourself so concerned with protecting what you have that it is hard, if not impossible, to invite exciting new projects and responsibilities into your life. Keep a wise balance between the two. Don't be greedy.

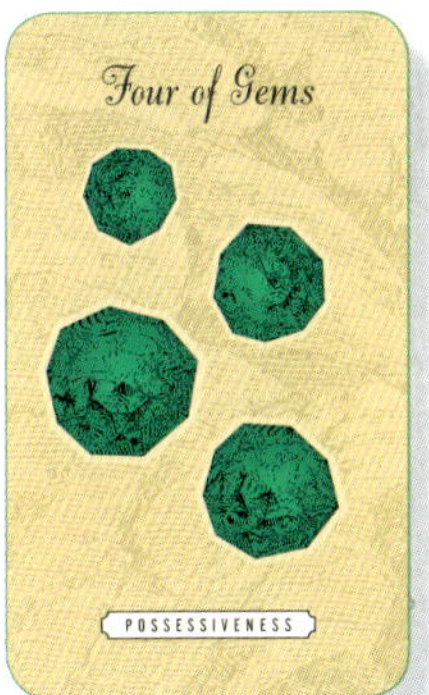

REVERSED

Quick Read: ***Guard against selfishness.***

• Nothing favorable can be gained from being greedy. If you truly value the positive things in your life, including the people you love, you will treat them with generosity. Do not mistake possessiveness for a way of showing love. Only a relationship that inspires spiritual growth and reflects your true values will endure. If you have that sort of union, fight to protect it. Remember that you must never treat people like objects. Not only will this attitude make you unpopular over time, but it unfairly diminishes the importance of the individuals in question as well.

• There is nothing wrong with holding on to who you have in your personal life. However, you should never try to recapture what is clearly gone. If a relationship is over, wish the person well and move on without anger or bitterness. Where money is concerned, it is perfectly legitimate to save for that proverbial rainy day, but don't hoard what you have.

Secret: Bear in mind the axiom "Money doesn't buy happiness." While you are right to value the resources that your enduring hard work and success have built, if you think riches alone are sufficient to bring joy, you are mistaken. Those who are cheap with money are cheap with love.

Five of Pentacles

KEYWORDS
• *Worries* • *Detour*
• *Anxiety* • *Distress*
• *Denial* • *Thrift*

UPRIGHT

Quick Read: ***Learn how to cope.***

• You need to control the level of anxiety you experience at this time. It may feel as if stress has taken over your life. Worries can paralyze all your actions if you aren't able to face their source, then focus on the present and do what you can with the here and now. If you let others know that this is a difficult time in your life, they will do what they can to help. Those who don't and who avoid you because of your problems are not really your friends.

• You might feel left out of the party—you may even feel ignored—but you should not waste time worrying about things in the past. A misunderstanding is best left just there—in the past. Obsessing about what was can keep you from living well, and happily, in the present.

Secret: Stress can be a great motivator, so long as you know how to use it to your advantage. Visualize yourself facing your worries—ask them what they're trying to protect you from and listen to what they have to say.

REVERSED

Quick Read: ***You may feel down and out.***

• If you are especially stressed-out and overwhelmed at this time, you might be experiencing a lack of support in a close personal relationship or in your workplace. If someone you care about is the individual who is going through a great deal of panic at this time, you may need to be the stabilizing force.

• If you are the individual in question, be aware of the fact that too much worry without corresponding action as an outlet can be extremely damaging to your health. At this point in your life you may find yourself so caught up in an ever-encroaching vortex of fear and panic that you have trouble navigating through all the demands of your path. You need to find what stability and comfort you can gain from close friends, family members, and colleagues, and use this support to help buck you up during this time.

Secret: Beware of your current level of anxiety. You may be experiencing actual panic attacks, which is a condition that requires treatment. Seek professional help for frightening, conflicting feelings and emotional upheavals that you may experience.

Six of Pentacles

KEYWORDS

• *Generosity* • *Investments*
• *Honesty* • *Sharing*
• *Resources* • *Charity*

UPRIGHT

Quick Read: ***Fulfillment comes from sharing.***

• You should be happy to know that this card suggests that you are currently surrounded by a spirit of generosity, sharing, and riches. You need to present yourself as a kind and charitable individual who is happy to help others. If you have recently been the recipient of someone else's generosity, you can repay this gift by passing it on to a person you know who needs your help.

• The wonderful thing about giving from your heart is that it increases your karmic credit. Of course, that should never be the only reason for generosity, but by doing good for others, you definitely increase the likelihood that the universe will be kind to you in return. Where romance is concerned, you will experience a mutual sharing of consideration and compassion. Continue to look on the bright side of life. It is a mark of spiritual good health.

Secret: This is a time when a wholly selfless action for someone you care about is not only a help to the individual in question but simply the right thing to do. Always keep in mind that positive actions have positive results. Your generosity, freely given, will come back to you tenfold.

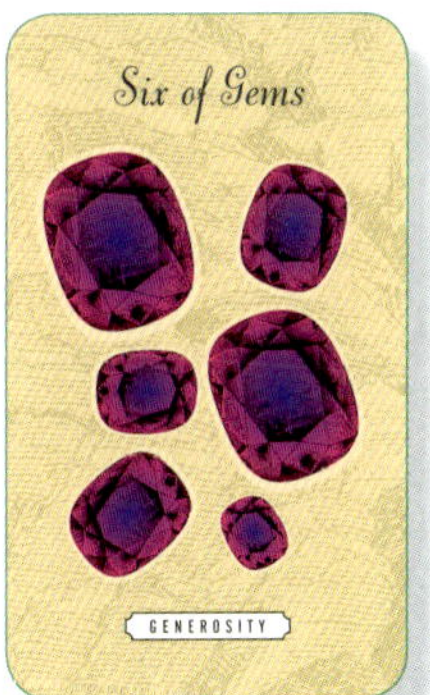

REVERSED

Quick Read: ***Don't be cheap or overly generous.***

• One of your chief concerns at this time is that there may not be enough of life's good things to go around. It might feel as if the generosity you have shown to others in the past is not being properly reciprocated. Alternatively, it is possible that the person you helped is selfish and unable to share.

• You could be feeling depressed because some of your much-cherished dreams have failed to materialize, despite your own best intentions. If you have withheld help from someone in the past, it is likely that you could be experiencing a sense of guilt or disappointment. Feeling deprived or being cheap creates bad karma for the future. What you put out into the universe comes back to you—and if you give very little, it is certain that you will get very little, or even less, in return.

Secret: Even though you want to be helpful to someone in need, you should guard against allowing yourself to be used by a demanding or needy person. This individual may be jealous of you because of his or her own unfulfilled dreams. Be discerning but not cheap.

Seven of Pentacles

KEYWORDS

• Frustration • Expectations • Pause • Interruption • Apprehension • Disappointment

UPRIGHT

Quick Read: ***Peace begins when expectations end.***

• This is not a time to overreach on your goals. Even though it is wise to do such things as save for a house, education, or retirement, a current financial crunch could make that difficult. Don't let minor frustrations keep you from making plans for the future. Seek attainable goals. Give thanks for the good things that are already in your life. If you can remember to be grateful for what is positive in your life, you are sure to triumph eventually.

• At this time you must maintain a strong and determined desire to achieve. Focus on the present and do what you can with what you have now. It is possible that more hard work will be necessary before you see results from your labors. Stay clear of an aggravating or frustrating person who could try your patience.

Secret: In order to deal with your frustrations about current goals, it helps to visualize all your past accomplishments. See the many times you worried that you would never attain them. Realize that you have more power now to be patient and resilient in the face of setbacks.

REVERSED

Quick Read: ***Broken promises cause problems.***

• When the Seven of Pentacles is reversed, it means that whatever you expected to happen was unreasonable. Remember, life holds no guarantees. What can hurt the most is that you can't expect some people close to you to keep their promises. Whether this is due to mischief making on their part, or merely a sense of them falling out of favor with your point of view, you are likely to feel hurt and bewildered because of their actions.

• One of your other greatest sources of frustration at this time could be the fact that you don't have the resources you need to make things happen. It is easy to be afraid of failing now, to the point where you may even be timid about trying too hard. Your attitude could be "I'm not going to make it, so why should I put my effort into this?" Try to stay away from that kind of thinking, however, because cynicism will only make it harder for you to accomplish your goals.

Secret: To get past the annoyance of frustration, you need to admit a few things. Frustration results from feeling ungrateful or impotent. You may believe that your best efforts often go unappreciated. A particularly frustrating or cynical person could be a factor now.

Eight of Pentacles

KEYWORDS

• *Craftsmanship* • *Study* • *Diligence* • *Expertise* • *Skill* • *Dedication*

UPRIGHT

Quick Read: ***Do your best.***

• If you are careful, practiced, and methodical, you will succeed. This is true regarding your creative life as well as in your relationships. If you study and analyze the fine points of the situation in order to make the best choices, your partnership or endeavor is sure to prosper. It is also a good idea to approach your relationship in the same way that a skilled craftsman would approach a project.

• There is nothing quite as satisfying as the feeling you get when you give a job your very best effort. The message from this card is about applying yourself and treating every aspect of your life with care, creativity, and professionalism. It is important that you present yourself as a skilled and dedicated person who takes enormous pride in your work. Let others see your great attention to detail without coming off as obsessive. You have mastered many skills.

Secret: Perfectionism may seem like a good thing, but now you would be better off avoiding it and looking instead to just getting the job done well. Dedicate yourself to using your talents and skills. Someone who has a finicky or perfectionist personality could come into your life at this time.

REVERSED

Quick Read: ***Perfectionism blocks progress.***

• When it comes to an important project, you need to pay attention to everything that goes into it, taking one step at a time rather than just looking at the end result. You have the opportunity to make some additional money at this time, though you should not concentrate solely on that fact since it is likely to be a small amount. Don't be afraid that your project won't be perfect; just do the very best that you can.

• If a relationship is currently in play, you can make things even better than they have been by focusing on the positive aspects of the union instead of worrying about what is wrong or what could go wrong. If your mate or lover is an overly critical individual, try to make him or her realize that being too much of a perfectionist can put undue stress and strain on the relationship, making things difficult for both of you.

Secret: Avoid being the kind of person who is more concerned with what is wrong than with what is right. It may be tempting to criticize or nitpick, but that is a negative approach to life, and you need positive energy. You may also tend to procrastinate and be blocked by perfectionism.

Nine of Pentacles

KEYWORDS

• Abundance • Health
• Independence
• Self-reliance
• Naturalness • Gain

UPRIGHT

Quick Read: ***Feel healthy, wealthy, and wise.***

• It is time for you to treat your health as you treat financial abundance—with care, respect, and consistent consideration. These are your premiere assets and must be protected at all costs. You can achieve the success you are looking for so long as you stress independence. Show others that you are an abundant source of ideas, inspiration, and wisdom and that you have accomplished what you set out to do.

• If you are looking for inspiration, you could find it outdoors. This is a great time for you to get out into the natural world and enjoy all that it has to offer. Look into the connection between nature and healing. You can gain valuable wisdom from tapping into the natural world. Do not make things too complicated. In most cases, in simplicity you will find truth.

Secret: Enjoy the independence you have earned. Because abundance of all descriptions is a factor in your life now, you need to guard against adding a few inches to your waistline. If you want to keep fit, you will need to exercise as well as eat right.

REVERSED

Quick Read: ***Let nature be your guide.***

• Independence is a vital issue in your life now, and if you don't assert yourself in this way, you are not going to make the gains for success you have been looking for. There is also a chance that you or a partner may be too independent. True love means wanting your partner to feel safe and secure enough to be his or her own person. This is true for you, as well. There is nothing wrong in asking for help.

• If you actually do have a great deal of abundance in your life at this time, you may find it hard or even impossible to identify with people who have a great deal less. If you don't have the sort of abundance you think you deserve, you may feel resentful. This attitude makes it even harder to make good things happen. Whatever your mood may be, don't just sit at home feeling sorry for yourself. Get moving and get out there.

Secret: It is not necessary to take the high-tech approach to staying healthy. A better way is to get out in the world and rediscover nature. Take walks and commune with the beauty of the outdoors. Inspiration for getting what you need will most likely come from being by yourself.

Ten of Pentacles

KEYWORDS
• Protection • Perfection
• Security • Status
• Influence • Heritage

UPRIGHT

Quick Read: *You are protected.*

• Drawing this card in a reading ensures that seeds that you planted in the past will bear fruit now. You will soon find yourself supported and protected by established rules and structures, and you can use this security to bolster your wealth, status, and influence. A conservative approach to your life has brought you to this point, so do not suddenly start gambling. Present yourself as successful and respectful of rich traditions, and continue to build on these strengths.

• There is a powerful circle of support around you now, a foundation you have built over the past few years. This is the ideal time to make important choices because you are sure to exercise common sense. Where romance is concerned, this card is an excellent sign. It indicates that a relationship of long standing can grow stronger, withstanding the test of time.

Secret: At this point you could find yourself feeling that you have achieved the status and influence that you deserve. You are upholding your family's heritage in the way you were meant to do. You are financially protected, so know that what you have worked to build is secure.

REVERSED

Quick Read: *Family ties can sometimes bind.*

• Despite the security you have in some quarters, you can't help feeling vulnerable and somewhat unprotected in other ways. For example, though your financial circumstances might be favorable, you could feel as if one of your relationships is on shaky ground. If you have too much of a protective influence surrounding you, there is a chance that you could be emotionally remote, removed from valuable life experiences.

• It is likely that you want all the advantages that come with money and social acceptance but fear the burdens that come as a result. Keep in mind that it can be hard to deal with these things, especially if you worry too much about how other people judge your actions or ideas. Remember that you should never be irresponsible with these resources or allow luxury or excess time to make you lazy. Prove to the universe that you are fully deserving of these great blessings by being responsible and conservative.

Secret: Your family or reputation could be a drawback to you now, or you could find yourself smothered by the overprotective opinions of a family member. Perhaps you may believe that you fall short of a parent's or sibling's example. Don't worry so much about what others think.

Princess (or Page) of Pentacles

KEYWORDS

- *Practicality* • *Techniques*
- *Commercial* • *Information*
- *Productivity*
- *Common sense*

UPRIGHT

Quick Read: ***The practical approach is best.***

• You aren't afraid to let others see that you are in tune with "just plain folks," although this could make you seem somewhat naive and unsophisticated. You don't mind getting your hands dirty because you know that is the way to accomplish what you want done. This is a time to persevere, use common sense, and trust your instincts. Right now you favor sensible, helpful projects such as yard work, home renovation, or crafts. This is a period when you are focused on gain, not glamour.

• You need to become even more aware of the natural rhythms and cycles in your life. The presence of this card in a reading may suggest that you will soon meet or become involved with an individual who has a talent for communicating useful information. A new friendship is likely to be extremely sincere and down-to-earth.

Secret: Others think you are moving too slowly on a project, but it is important that you take a deliberate and steady approach. Work and career matters are the focus of your life now; a business acquaintance could become a closer friend now. You may be starting a new business.

REVERSED

Quick Read: ***Improve your skills.***

• You may worry that you don't have enough real-life experience to solve a current dilemma. Perhaps you give up too easily. You might have lost out on something important, perhaps due to a lack of imagination. You need to draw on the skills that you *do* have—diligence, common sense, and a good work ethic—to carry you through to commercial success and material achievement.

• You may be involved with an extremely practical person who seems to be cramping your style. It is also possible that someone you love, perhaps a new or existing partner, could be unkempt, uncouth, or even antagonistic to your way of enjoying life. If you are currently unattached, it is possible that in the very near future you could become involved with someone younger, or perhaps somebody who works with you will become a love interest.

Secret: You have a great gift for communication, so this is not the time to withdraw into silence just because you are afraid others might see you as naive. Don't be afraid to ask questions if you don't understanding something. Keep honing your skills.

Prince (or Knight) of Pentacles

KEYWORDS

- Trustworthiness
- Reliability • Business
- Seriousness • Fixation
- Responsibility

UPRIGHT

Quick Read: ***Plant seeds for the future.***

• This card suggests that hard work, sound investments, and accumulating a sizable nest egg are of singular importance to you now. If this card depicts not you but someone else, there is a chance that you work or will work with this person or may entrust him or her with a business proposition that is valuable to you. If you are the person who must conduct business with another, show that person that you have high scruples and can be trusted and relied on.

• In regard to relationships, you could find yourself involved with a strong-minded, determined, and rather stubborn individual. This is a serious person, and it could take time for the heart of this reliable, good provider to open. Show others that you value responsibility and common sense. Since you are looking for steadiness and purpose now, it is unlikely that you will get involved in a hot affair or a get-rich-quick scheme.

Secret: Show others that you can be reliable and consistent. Take your business dealings forward one small step at a time. Do not allow yourself to be fixated on wealth. Financial good fortune is part of the plan but shouldn't represent the grand design of a successful life.

REVERSED

Quick Read: ***Beware of political gamesmanship.***

• Soon you could meet someone who has the characteristics of the Prince of Pentacles. You might meet while the two of you are working together or are engaged in some form of business. While this person is highly capable, there is a likelihood that he will try to exert too much control over your enterprise.

• You should pay attention to your own priorities now. Don't let ruthless ambition govern your life. Unless you believe in the life, work, or causes you are espousing, you are unlikely to achieve lasting success. Remember, being good with money is likely to be one of your strong points, but you don't want to be seen by others as being miserly or controlling.

Secret: Be aware of the fact that if someone is cheap with money, he or she is likely to be cheap with love, too. You do not need this type of individual in your life, especially if you are an exceptionally giving person.

Queen of Pentacles

KEYWORDS

• *Good fortune* • *Patronage* • *Influence* • *Affluence* • *Results* • *Profit*

UPRIGHT

Quick Read: ***Gratitude is the best attitude.***

• Your key issue now is being able to protect your good fortune and that of the people who matter so much to you. Show that you have the ability to communicate with others in a straightforward manner yet are passive enough to be receptive to their needs. Do not be put off by the fact that others may see you as privileged, even elitist. You know how to use your great abundance to help others.

• This is a time to be aware of the financial problems of those less fortunate than you. You can help and nurture someone who dearly needs your assistance now. To safeguard what you have, try visualizing yourself as the ruler of a kingdom, able to use your power and influence to do good works. It is also time to be enchanted. Live life to the fullest—appreciate the gifts of beauty, love, and grace all around you! Socialize and spread good cheer.

Secret: If you are not a patron of the arts, it's time to become one. Attending social events can provide you with important connections that you could profit from. There is also a strong possibility that a wealthy and influential person could enter your life. Enjoy your good fortune.

REVERSED

Quick Read: ***Take nothing for granted.***

• When the Queen of Pentacles is reversed, it generally depicts a haughty individual who has the ability to behave like an aristocratic snob. If these attitudes in any way describe you, it is high time to make some important changes. Stop judging other people by what material goods and financial success they have and instead appreciate them for who they are inside.

• While this is a time for socializing, you also need to be aware of the fact that there is another more valuable world beyond that of parties and social enclaves. If you are not this type of person, you may be close to someone who is. You could fear becoming desensitized to people who have far less than you do. You could be in danger of forfeiting your humanity unless you are willing to investigate how the less fortunate live.

Secret: An obsessive need for privacy is an issue for you now. A need to protect your privacy can lead you to be emotionally cold and insensitive to others. You may believe, in error, that people are envious of you.

King of Pentacles

KEYWORDS

• *Pragmatism* • *Worth*
• *Prosperity* • *Earthiness*
• *Budget* • *Instincts*

UPRIGHT

Quick Read: ***Be the boss.***

• It's time to get down to basics. Be yourself, whoever that might be. Show others that you have it all together. Your commonsense, political approach will get you where you want to go, so stick to your practical instincts. There may be individuals who feel as if you are taking the easy way out of a situation—but you know it is more about getting along with others and playing the percentages than about looking like you are the smartest kid in the class.

• It is equally important that you maintain your ties to the people you know and trust. Looking outside your circle is not advised at this time, because the more grounded you remain, the better off you will be. If you have the opportunity to become a deal maker in the days or weeks to come, take advantage of it. There is money to be made.

Secret: Your chance for financial gain is good now. Either you will have good luck with money or you will be able to attract the attention of and receive help from someone who is highly skilled in financial matters, possibly a pragmatic type of person with an earthy sense of humor.

REVERSED

Quick Read: ***Don't rest on your laurels.***

• If you or someone you love embodies the humble and earthy qualities of the King of Pentacles, you can expect this important relationship to become stalled, repetitive, and downright boring. It is also possible that someone you love could possess attitudes, habits, or even annoying quirks that make being together difficult. Money worries and budget crunches could be adding to the problem.

• Sometimes, the King of Pentacles reversed can signify a misguided search for what is true and real, leading you to have foolish expectations. In a relationship, either romantic or platonic, you may be the one who is well connected or well-heeled. As a result, you may feel as if you are liked only for what you possess. Being unsure of who you are, what you represent, and why you represent it can be just one of the dilemmas you face in a relationship at this time.

Secret: Try not to be narrow-minded or provincial. Following traditional aims is good, so far as it goes, but if you resist something new simply because you've got cold feet, you'll end up being sorry. You should never be afraid to be bold. Prejudice could be a problem now.

How to Do a Multicard Reading

Now that you have done enough one-card readings to feel comfortable with your basic understanding of the cards, it's time to step up to the next level.

To lay the cards out in a spread, you will take cards, one at a time, in sequence, from the top of the pile of seventy-eight cards and place them face up in your chosen layout.

The Tarot is usually consulted when we seek an answer to a specific question or when we need guidance for a particular problem or challenge. A Tarot spread is a method of laying out the cards in a specific pattern. There are numerous types of spreads with patterns that involve varying numbers of cards. The position of each card in a spread has an essential meaning to the interpretation of the entire pattern.

The more card readings you do, the easier it will become for you to piece together a consecutive story and relate the cards that appear in particular spreads to one another. Sample readings and interpretation examples are provided for each spread.

THE TWELVE MASTER SPREADS

Once you have become familiar with the cards by pulling one card in answer to a question, you are ready to learn how to do your first Tarot spread. The challenge of doing multicard readings is the necessity of interpreting a particular card in terms of its position in the spread. Each position in a spread represents a specific aspect of your multidimensional answer. This is where your creativity comes into play.

Obviously, we do not have space in this book to interpret each card for each of the ninety-two positions possible in the twelve spreads. You need to read the meaning of the card occupying a particular position of a spread—upright or reversed—in the context of the position it occupies. The meaning you interpret for a particular card in the Mind position of the Mind-Body-Spirit spread should be different from the meaning you interpret for it if it occupies the Body or Spirit position. We give specific examples of how to read the various positions of each of the twelve spreads, so don't worry. It takes a little getting used to, but it's worth it.

Once you feel comfortable with your ability to interpret the cards in the context of their position in a Mind-Body-Spirit spread, you can move on to any of the multiple-card spreads. We recommend that you do so in the following order.

The variety of special spreads we offer you here, along with the secrets of the card symbols, upright and reversed, lead you to understand and experience more meaning from the forces that affect you, while offering solutions to important issues and answers to specific questions.

With practice, you will discover in yourself unsuspected psychic gifts to help yourself and to help others navigate through and gain insight on their life path.

Now it's time for the twelve Master Spreads of Tarot Secrets. It's all you need to know to read Tarot like a pro!

1 MIND-BODY-SPIRIT SPREAD

This three-card spread offers advice on how one's mind, body, and spirit are affected in the present moment, and what to do about it.

2 LAW OF ATTRACTION SPREAD

Every spiritual seeker must face the fears and obstacles that prevent him or her from going on to the next level, and this four-card spread is the reading that can help you do so and therefore begin to manifest your goals.

3 PAST-PRESENT-FUTURE SPREAD

This four-card spread describes and analyzes the progression of any situation, what went wrong and what went right, and how things are destined to be unless you make the suggested changes.

4 CHAKRA SPREAD

This seven-card spread describes the seven energy centers of one's body, where universal life force enters and energizes us. Learn how you're processing the energy the universe is trying to give you and how to best make use of it.

5 THE LUCKY HORSESHOE SPREAD

This seven-card spread is helpful for those who want a straightforward reading that will give quick insights into seven important aspects of your life.

6 WISH UPON A STAR SPREAD

This seven-card spread will show you the lessons and surprises that will come when you make a wish, and the particular influences surrounding that experience.

7 RELATIONSHIP SPREAD

This eight-card spread explains the dynamics in any relationship or business situation and provides insight into the energies at the present moment.

8 SPIRITUAL GROWTH SPREAD

This nine-card spread is a spiritual snapshot with advice on how to make the most of your situation for your personal soul development.

9 TREE OF LIFE SPREAD

This mystical spread is based on the Kabbalah and the Tree of Life. It is a ten-card spread that shows life-cycle patterns, highlights the wisdom we accrue and take with us on our path, and inspires us to use our unique talents to better ourselves and the world around us.

10 MAGIC MANDALA SPREAD

This ten-card meditation spread reveals a complete picture of you and the energies surrounding you.

11 CELTIC CROSS SPREAD

The most familiar of Tarot readings is the perfect eleven-card spread for the most detailed analysis of any situation.

12 ZODIAC WHEEL SPREAD

This twelve-card spread identifies the twelve most important issues affecting the twelve most important areas of one's life at the present moment.

Mind-Body-Spirit Spread

THREE CARDS

This simple three-card spread gives a quick overview to reflect how you are balanced in your life now—mentally, physically, and spiritually.

Ask: "How will doing ______ affect me?" or "If I choose to ______, describe the influences on my mind, body, and spirit."

Shuffle and cut the Tarot deck, and lay out three cards in a row from left to right.

The cards represent your mind, or mental attitude (card 1), your body, or physical manifestation of the question (card 2), and your spirit, or how the question affects your heart and soul (card 3). The Mind position relates to your experience of communications and can include thoughts and ideas. The Body position speaks of the here and now, what is happening physically around you right now. The Spirit position relates to how the question affects your spirit if you continue on the current path.

1	2	3

SAMPLE MIND-BODY-SPIRIT SPREAD

Question: *"Where am I right now—mentally, physically, and spiritually?"*

In this case we are using the main interpretation of each card to read the spread.

1 WHAT'S ON YOUR MIND

14 Temperance

Say good-bye to extremes of all sorts. This card denotes the importance of moderation in all circumstances. Now is not the time to be impetuous in any area of your life. A slow, measured, and well-considered approach is what you need in order to be successful at this point in time.

This doesn't mean you should be afraid to experiment—but keep the importance of prioritization constantly before you. An incident or personal matter is likely to require more restraint than you are accustomed to displaying. Even if this situation is more complex than you originally perceived it to be, don't rush your response, because it could be detrimental. Instead, channel your energy in a way that promotes a slow and steady approach, such as making comprehensive lists of what you want and what you don't want—and the steps you need to take in order to ensure both.

2 HOW YOUR BODY FEELS

Six of Wands

It is no wonder that you feel like a winner—you are one! The spotlight is on you at this time, indicating a gratifying period in your life. With so much energy and excitement at your disposal, you are charged with charisma and eager to make important decisions about your future. You should use a current victory to build a foundation for future successes.

You also need to realize that just because everything is going your way now does not mean that it will do so forever. Therefore, enjoy your success while it is at hand, and do not take it for granted. If you are merely on the brink of a new victory, you can presume that the outcome will turn out positively for you. When that victory comes, you need to accept the time of recognition as something you deserve and have worked hard to attain.

3 YOUR SPIRITUAL ESSENCE

Princess (or Page) of Wands (reversed)

One of the hallmarks of youth is immaturity. This may describe you, someone who is part of your life now, or someone who is about to join your circle. You may have to deal with the characteristic recklessness of a young person or put up with an immature friend's antics. Whether or not these traits are a part of your own character, you need to beware of being annoying, speaking carelessly, or being hotheaded.

A lack of spontaneity or eagerness can be equally self-defeating. There is no shame in being inexperienced, so long as you are open to gaining wisdom and experience in whatever way the universe sees fit to bestow it. Your challenge at this time is to keep from appearing as if you are indiscreet, imprudent, or foolish. This means you need to refrain from spreading gossip or rumors of any kind. Be more aware of developing your social skills. By the same token, beware of doing too much socializing, especially with people who don't really matter to you.

Law of Attraction Spread

FOUR CARDS

The Law of Attraction Spread is a four-card spread designed to give you the necessary direction to determine how to reach your goals. It can be used to assess a goal and the steps needed to manifest this goal, as well as to help identify those things that may get in the way of achieving the goal. You might ask "What can help me manifest my dream of getting my book published?" or "How can I best meet my perfect mate?"

CARD POSITIONS

CARD 1

Identifying the goal and your first step

CARD 2

Qualities that can aid in achieving the goal

CARD 3

Obstacles in the way of manifestation

CARD 4

Best visualization to achieve the goal

SAMPLE LAW OF ATTRACTION SPREAD

Sample question: *"How can I manifest having a better relationship with my sister Susan?"*

In this example we are using the second paragraph of each card's interpretation to form the answers to each position of the spread.

1 IDENTIFYING THE GOAL AND YOUR FIRST STEP

Ace of Swords (reversed)

Beware of instituting a self-fulfilling prophecy. For instance, if you fear that you or someone close to you is not up to a challenge, you are virtually giving such a negative thought the power to come true. If you are not sure about speaking your mind because of how your words will be received, keep silent.

2 QUALITIES THAT CAN AID IN ACHIEVING THE GOAL

21 The World (reversed)

Make certain that the world you are about to enter allows the freedom of choice you are looking for and deserve. It might be tempting to frame your aspirations according to what a mate, parent, or mentor expects of you. This is your life, so it is up to you to handle it in a way that best makes you feel whole. It may take a while, but you will learn how to put your learning experiences into perspective.

3 OBSTACLES IN THE WAY OF MANIFESTATION

Prince (or Knight) of Swords

You may have the opportunity to act in the role of teacher or mentor to a younger, less-experienced individual. As a matter of fact, you could find yourself magnetically drawn to an individual because of his or her intellect and openness. If there is an opportunity to get behind a cause that is dear to your heart, you can be expected to draw other people to your banner. Dreams have the opportunity to become solid reality now. Try to be more reflective and studious and you can reach your goals.

4 BEST VISUALIZATION TO ACHIEVE THE GOAL

Eight of Wands

You may be feeling exceptionally tuned-in to a wonderful person at this time. In order to make this relationship (whether it be romance, friendship, or creative partnership) work, you need to be totally honest about your feelings. Don't expect the other person to read your mind. Even if verbal communication isn't your thing, make an effort to speak your mind. Be clear, concise, and to the point.

Past-Present-Future Spread

FOUR CARDS

One of the best spreads for a simple yes-or-no question is this four-card Tarot spread. If you were wondering about your business situation and your question was something like "Should I hire this person I am considering?" then the Past-Present-Future Spread is a great layout to use.

With this spread, four cards are chosen and laid out in a straight horizontal line. Shuffle, cut, and choose your cards. Allow your mind to relax, and let your intuition weave the meaning of these four cards together. Read the energies of each in turn; then blend these meanings together to give a whole picture.

CARD POSITIONS

CARD 1

The past: *the background or history behind this issue*

CARD 2

The present: *what is currently happening and influencing this issue*

CARD 3

The future: *all the coming choices and influences that will impact this issue*

CARD 4

The outcome: *what will most likely occur, provided you continue on the path you are on*

SAMPLE PAST-PRESENT-FUTURE SPREAD

Sample question: *"Should I go back to school?"*

In this example we are reading the Secrets of each card in each position to do the reading.

1 THE PAST: the background or history behind this issue

4 The Emperor

Secret: Because you don't hide the fact that you want to achieve power, others might see you as cold, even ruthless. But people who support your climb to the top see only your charismatic and powerful personality.

2 THE PRESENT: what is currently happening and influencing this issue

19 The Sun (reversed)

Secret: It may be time to question whether or not you have developed the sense of independence you need in order to be happy and successful. It is likely that a parent or other authority figure is pressuring you unfairly, and you may feel it as a blow to your ego.

3 THE FUTURE: all the coming choices and influences that will impact this issue

Ten of Wands

Secret: Learn to identify whether or not you are a workaholic. If you bend all of your energy toward work instead of personal relationships, you probably are. It is time to bring more balance into your life. Take a time-out.

4 THE OUTCOME: what will most likely occur, provided you continue on the path you are on

Seven of Cups

Secret: There is a possibility that your idealization of an individual or an idea has blinded you to the faults of this person or the pitfalls that your fantasy may actually have. Rather than deceiving yourself, be willing to see the truth. Know that you have alternatives.

Chakra Spread

SEVEN CARDS

Chakra is the word for "wheel" or "disk" in the strange but beautiful Sanskrit language of India, one of the most ancient languages known. The concept of our personal chakras comes from yoga and refers to the seven spinning disks of colored light that experienced yogis report seeing in their mind's eye during deep meditation. The chakras always occur at specific points from the base of the spine to the crown of the head. We think of the chakras as seven round energy "doorways" along our spine connecting us to the universal life force.

Our Chakra Spread is designed to recharge and refresh. This spread is useful when you are looking for a healing, balancing, meditative Tarot session. The card you pick for each chakra will give insight into how the issue concerning you can be addressed from the perspective of balancing the energies of your charkas and how the energies represented by that chakra are manifesting for you in the present moment. Shuffle and draw seven cards, placing them one at a time in the spread diagrammed at right.

1 ROOT CHAKRA

What is the root of, or the basis for, your problem? How vital and energetic are you? What habits are you tied into?

The First or Root Chakra, located at the base of the spine near the coccyx, is the source of our powerful, primal life energy. The card you pick indicates what areas in life are affecting your sense of security, how you relate to the physical world, and what materialistic issues you are presently working on. This chakra forms our foundation and is related to our survival instincts and to our sense of grounding and connection to our bodies and the physical plane. Ideally this chakra brings us health, prosperity, and security.

2 SPLEEN CHAKRA

How are you using your sexual or creative energy? What emotions are you feeling deeply? What are you trying to assimilate or take in?

The Second or Spleen Chakra is located in the lower back and reproductive organs and is associated with our sexuality and creativity. The card you pick describes issues that are affecting your emotional well-being and sex life, and what lessons you need to learn concerning the deeply felt relationships you have. The Second Chakra connects us to others through desire, sensation, and movement. Ideally this chakra brings us fluidity and grace, depth of feeling, sexual fulfillment, and the ability to accept change.

3 NAVEL CHAKRA

Who or what are you strongly connected to? What convictions do you hold?

The Third or Navel Chakra is located in the solar plexus and is connected to our self-assertion as we shape and expand our being in the world. The card you pick describes issues affecting your ability to stay centered and shows what circumstances you need to be aware of that have the potential to affect your life. This chakra is also known as the Power Chakra. It rules the will, and, when balanced, this chakra brings us energy, effectiveness, and spontaneity.

4 HEART CHAKRA

What is your ability to heal yourself? Is your heart in it? What is the key to your healing process? What must you accept with unconditional love?

The Fourth or Heart Chakra has to do with your ability to give and receive love. The card in this position can describe what areas we need to show empathy in and what lessons we must encounter in learning to trust more.

The Fourth Chakra is connected to our ability to love and our ability to feel the love of others for us. This chakra is the middle chakra in a system of seven. A balanced Fourth Chakra allows us to feel compassion and have a deep sense of peace and centeredness.

5 THROAT CHAKRA

What does your unconscious or inner self have to say? What are you actually communicating? How are you expressing yourself?

The Fifth Chakra is located in the throat and is thus related to communication and creativity. Here we experience the world symbolically through vibration, such as the vibration of sound representing language. This chakra is associated with communication, knowledge, and self-expression.

The Throat Chakra has to do with areas we need to listen carefully to, as well as our true message when speaking or writing. The card in this position can also describe relationships with those who stimulate our ability to communicate.

6 BROW CHAKRA

What are your visions or intuition telling you? What possibilities are you seeing?

The Sixth Chakra is located in the brow at the point where many spiritual people say our third eye is located and serves to connect us directly to all other beings through compassionate, holistic thought and psychic communication.

The card you select indicates what areas of life you need to take a closer look at and how those areas can help you use your imagination to expand your creativity. This chakra is related to the act of seeing, both physically and intuitively. As such, it opens our psychic faculties and our understanding of archetypal levels. When balanced, it allows us to see clearly, in effect letting us see "the big picture."

7 CROWN CHAKRA

What will be the next step in your spiritual growth? What can assist you in your process of becoming wiser?

The Seventh or Crown Chakra is located at the top of the head. Besides serving as our connection to the energy of the universe, it is connected with our devotion and identification with causes and forces beyond our individual selves. The card you select can show how your spirituality is developing and what obstacles are keeping you from fully connecting to your Higher Self.

The Crown Chakra is associated with our connection to the greater world beyond, to a timeless, universal place of all knowing. When balanced, this chakra brings us knowledge, wisdom, understanding, spiritual connection, and bliss.

SAMPLE CHAKRA SPREAD

Shuffle and cut the Tarot deck, and choose seven cards while asking for guidance to balance your seven chakras. Then use the "Secret" section of each of the chosen cards to provide the reading. We cannot stress enough the importance of interpreting the answers in regard to the questions of each specific chakra.

You will notice that we start by reading the seventh position, the Crown Chakra, and then work our way down from the spiritual to and through the material levels. This symbolizes how we each draw down the limitless pure energy of the Divine and use it to animate ourselves and our world.

7 CROWN CHAKRA

What will be the next step in your spiritual growth? What can assist you in your process of becoming wiser?

Ace of Wands

Secret: In an effort to reveal your abilities, you will be involved in the initiation of a bold new project. There will be a breakthrough, and a testing of your nerve as well as your talent. When you take action, be determined and be direct.

6 BROW CHAKRA

What are your visions or intuition telling you? What possibilities are you seeing?

20 Judgment (reversed)

Secret: Your inner critic can render the strongest judgment of all at this time. You feel you were indecisive and didn't rise to a challenge correctly. Berating yourself for mistakes you might have made can undercut your self-esteem.

5 THROAT CHAKRA

What does your unconscious or inner self have to say? What are you actually communicating? How are you expressing yourself?

Prince (or Knight) of Pentacles (reversed)

Secret: Be aware of the fact that if someone is cheap with money, he or she is likely to be cheap with love, too. You do not need this type of individual in your life, especially if you are an exceptionally giving person.

4 HEART CHAKRA

What is your ability to heal yourself? Is your heart in it? What is the key to your healing process? What must you accept with unconditional love?

Four of Wands

Secret: Even if you are comfortable in your current course of action, you may worry about losing the foundation that you have worked so hard to attain. You need to trust more fully in the good fortune and good karma you've created. Give thanks.

3

NAVEL CHAKRA

Who or what are you strongly connected to? What convictions do you hold?

Ten of Swords

Secret: Because of your distress, it may seem that you have little, if anything, to live for or to give to others at this time. The answer to these feelings is realizing that you are actually far luckier than many other people. Keep that in mind. Sharing and articulating your pain can help to comfort you.

2

SPLEEN CHAKRA

How are you using your sexual or creative energy? What emotions are you feeling deeply? What are you trying to assimilate or take in?

6 The Lovers

Secret: It may be a time to make an important decision, but if romance or passion is concerned, make sure it is really what and whom you want. This card can represent a love affair but doesn't necessarily predict a permanent commitment.

1

ROOT CHAKRA

What is the root of, or the basis for, your problem? How vital and energetic are you? What habits are you tied into?

9 The Hermit (reversed)

Secret: A lack of social interaction or involvements can leave you feeling disconnected from those in your circle. Friends might feel neglected by you, and you might experience occasional bouts of depression or loneliness.

Lucky Horseshoe Spread

SEVEN CARDS

There are seven cards in this spread, which is good for getting a feeling for how your luck is running with regard to a specific question. We agree with America's third president, Thomas Jefferson, who said, "I'm a great believer in luck and I find the harder I work the more I have of it," but sometimes hard work and preparation need a bit of luck to accomplish a goal.

Ask a specific question, such as "How will my luck run if I switch jobs this year?" or "Describe how my luck will run if I choose to _______."

After you have shuffled and cut, lay out the cards to form the horseshoe-shaped spread according to the diagram. Begin with card 1: Turn it over, read and interpret it, and then, in sequence, do the same with each card until all have been read. The positions and meanings of each card are as follows.

CARD POSITIONS

1 PAST

The immediate past, or further back in time. It describes attitudes and issues that inform your current situation. This card will assist you in identifying what went wrong and help you work out how to right it.

2 PRESENT

Immediate present situation. This card may describe current actions, thoughts, and feelings, and the prevailing circumstances that are right around you. This card reveals things that are current, enabling you to plan the right next step.

3 FUTURE

Developments that are coming in the very near future. This card can describe fresh influences that may come into play, and if you put some thought into reading this card, you should be able to make some sense of it.

4 THE UNEXPECTED

Something revealed that could be on your mind. The unexpected card is often the key to the reading. It can describe the fears or concerns about the question, something you should be aware of.

5 ATTITUDE OF ANOTHER

This card is designed to identify outside influences. This will usually be a person known to you and somehow connected with the question. This card describes the actions and attitudes about this situation from other people around you.

6 OBSTACLE

If a favorable card comes up in this slot, it indicates that there is no real obstacle to overcome; if the card is unfavorable, it describes the type of obstacle you have to face. It can describe problems that must be dealt with and resolved.

7 OUTCOME

This card guides you to look into the future to predict how certain situations you are currently experiencing may eventually turn out. This will be the logical culmination of all the other cards in the Horseshoe Spread, or the most likely solution to your question.

SAMPLE HORSESHOE SPREAD

Sample question: *"Describe how my luck will run if I choose to move to Seattle."*

In this example we are reading the cards by looking only at the "Quick Read" section of each card's interpretation, except for the seventh card, the Outcome, for which you should read both the Quick Read and that card's Secret. Apply these answers to the meaning of each card position in the spread.

1

PAST

The immediate past, or further back in time. It describes attitudes and issues that inform your current situation. This card will assist you in identifying what went wrong and help you work out how to right it.

Six of Swords

Quick Read: *You've weathered the storm.*

2

PRESENT

Immediate present situation. This card may describe current actions, thoughts, and feelings, and the prevailing circumstances that are right around you. This card reveals things that are current, enabling you to plan the next right step.

Seven of Swords (reversed)

Quick Read: *Evaluate your opposition.*

3

FUTURE

Developments that are coming in the very near future. This card can describe fresh influences that may come into play, and if you put some thought into reading this card, you should be able to make some sense of it.

14 Temperance (reversed)

Quick Read: *Don't be too stubborn.*

4

THE UNEXPECTED

Something revealed that could be on your mind. The unexpected card is often the key to the reading. It can describe the fears or concerns about the question, something you should be aware of.

Three of Wands

Quick Read: *Opportunities abound.*

5

ATTITUDE OF ANOTHER

This card is designed to identify outside influences. This will usually be a person known to you and somehow connected with the question. This card describes the actions and attitudes about this situation from other people around you.

I The Magician

Quick Read: *You've got the power!*

6 OBSTACLE

If a favorable card comes up in this slot, it indicates that there is no real obstacle to overcome; if the card is unfavorable, it describes the type of obstacle you have to face. It can describe problems that must be dealt with and resolved.

King of Cups (reversed)

Quick Read: *Beware of addictive behavior.*

7 OUTCOME

This card guides you to look into the future to predict how certain situations you are currently experiencing may eventually turn out. This will be the logical culmination of all the other cards in the Horseshoe Spread, or the most likely solution to your question.

Four of Wands

Quick Read: *Count your blessings.*

Secret: Even if you are comfortable in your current course of action, you may worry about losing the foundation that you have worked so hard to attain. You need to trust more fully in the good fortune and good karma you've created. Give thanks.

Note: Read the Secret of the card in this position from the point of view of how your luck is going to run. In this case, it's telling you to trust in the good fortune and good karma you've created and give thanks. I would interpret this to mean that you are in luck!

Wish upon a Star Spread

SEVEN CARDS

This seven-card spread will show you the lessons and surprises that will come when you make a wish, and the particular influences surrounding that experience.

Make a wish and see what the cards have to say. Will you get your wish? If not, what positive steps can you take to make your wish come true? Ask about your heart's true desire. You might say, "I wish for a new career direction," "I wish to find a great place to live," "I wish to find my soul mate," or "I wish to make more money."

CARD POSITIONS

1 THE NATURE OF YOUR WISH

This card may confirm what you want. If it seems to disagree, it may give insight into what may be a key to helping you manifest your wish.

2 WHAT AFFECTS YOUR WISH IN A POSITIVE WAY

This card offers guidance about what can help in this situation to make your wish come true.

3 WHAT AFFECTS YOUR WISH IN A NEGATIVE WAY

This card shows what may intervene as an obstacle to getting your wish.

4 PAST INFLUENCES

This card shows the actions that were taken that affect your wish.

5 PRESENT INFLUENCES

This card brings your life into focus right now.

6 FUTURE INFLUENCES

This card looks at the near future and shows the direction your wish is currently taking.

7 FINAL OUTCOME

This card offers guidance and tells how best to achieve your rewards and success.

SAMPLE WISH UPON A STAR SPREAD

Sample wish: *"I wish I could make more money."*

In this example we use the Quick Read answers for each card. To have it make sense and work to give you the message you need to hear, make sure to apply the answer directly to the meaning of each card position in the spread.

1 THE NATURE OF YOUR WISH

This card may confirm what you want. If it seems to disagree, it may give insight into what may be a key to helping you manifest your wish.

Queen of Cups (reversed)

Quick Read: *Don't absorb the negativity of others.*

2 WHAT AFFECTS YOUR WISH IN A POSITIVE WAY

This card offers guidance about what can help in this situation to make your wish come true.

3 The Empress

Quick Read: *It's time for creativity.*

3 WHAT AFFECTS YOUR WISH IN A NEGATIVE WAY

This card shows what may intervene as an obstacle to getting your wish.

Eight of Swords (reversed)

Quick Read: *Indecision will cause problems.*

4 PAST INFLUENCES

This card shows the actions that were taken that affect your wish.

Princess (or Page) of Pentacles

Quick Read: *The practical approach is best.*

5 PRESENT INFLUENCES

This card brings your life into focus right now.

21 The World

Quick Read: *Graduation day has arrived.*

6 FUTURE INFLUENCES

This card looks at the near future and shows the direction your wish is currently taking.

Three of Swords (reversed)

Quick Read: *Care, but don't be careless.*

7 FINAL OUTCOME

This card offers guidance and tells how best to achieve your rewards and success.

Nine of Cups

Quick Read: *Your wish is granted!*

Relationship Spread

EIGHT CARDS

This eight-card spread is used when someone is searching for answers about a romantic relationship. It can also be used for friendship or family relationships. It shows what you desire, troubles in your relationship, where you need help, what course the relationship is on, and what the potential end result is if you continue on that course.

Say: "Describe the nature of my relationship with ______ at this time," "Give me perspective on the vibes in this relationship," or "I need guidance for my love life."

This spread uses a total of eight cards. Shuffle, cut, and spread the cards out in a long fan. Pull the eight cards, one at a time, and place them in the spread, following the diagram.

CARD 1

The first card is laid at the top, in front of the person receiving the reading.

CARD 2

Card 2 is laid underneath and to the left of card 1.

CARD 3

Card 3 is laid to the right of card 2. This sets up a triangle, and you'll build two columns in descending order from cards 2 and 3.

CARDS 4 AND 6

Beneath card 2, you will lay your fourth and sixth cards drawn from the deck.

CARDS 5 AND 7

Beneath card 3, you will lay your fifth and seventh cards drawn.

CARD 6

The eighth and final card is laid at the bottom of the columns in a position similar to card 1, only this time it's in front of the person giving the reading.

CARD POSITIONS

1 How the person receiving the reading perceives him- or herself

2 How the person receiving the reading views his or her partner

3 The conditions surrounding the relationship at the present time

4 The person's needs in the relationship

5 What the person means to his or her partner

6 Problems and difficulties in the relationship

7 The strong points of the relationship

8 What will potentially happen within the relationship

SAMPLE RELATIONSHIP SPREAD

Sample question: *"Describe the nature of my relationship with Sam."*

In this case the querent chose to read the Keywords given for each card. When reading the Keywords as your answer, it doesn't matter if the cards are upright or reversed. Keep in mind that there will usually be at least one of the keywords for each card that directly "speak" to you and describe the situation that each card and card position addresses. If none of the keywords seem to describe the situation, you will have to read the entire meaning of that card.

1 How the person receiving the reading perceives him- or herself

2 The High Priestess

Keywords: *Intuition • Receptivity • Knowing • Philosophy • Femininity • Meditation*

2 How the person receiving the reading views his or her partner

Ten of Pentacles

Keywords: *Protection • Perfection • Security • Status • Influence • Heritage*

3 The conditions surrounding the relationship at the present time

Six of Wands

Keywords: *Victory • Applause • Approval • Endorsement • Transcendence • Adjustments*

4 The person's needs in the relationship

Three of Pentacles

Keywords: *Work • Production • Artistry • Consideration • Business • Conscientiousness*

5 What the person means to his or her partner

II Justice

Keywords: *Truth • Structure • Paperwork • Adjustment • Morality • Legal matters*

6 Problems and difficulties in the relationship

Seven of Cups

Keywords: *Illusion • Wishes • Escapism • Fantasy • Vacillation • Misconception*

7 The strong points of the relationship

Two of Swords

Keywords: *Balance • Alternatives • Rest • Withdrawal • Diplomacy • Compromise*

8 What will potentially happen within the relationship

King of Wands

Keywords: *Dynamism • Actions • Idealism • Keenness • Analysis • Leadership*

Spiritual Growth Spread

NINE CARDS

This nine-card spread is used when the person receiving the reading is looking to grow emotionally and spiritually. It describes where you are now, your goals, your positive points, the underlying problem, and the best way to proceed in order to carry out the advice given, and offers spiritual guidance concerning your desires for the future.

Ask: "Give me insight into my life right now so I can learn and grow" or "I request spiritual guidance for my highest good and greatest joy."

This diamond layout uses a total of nine cards. Shuffle, cut, and lay your cards out in order, and you should wind up with the following pattern:

TOP ROW

Card 9 centered

SECOND ROW FROM THE TOP

Cards 8 and 2, building a triangle with card 9

THIRD ROW FROM THE TOP

Cards 7, 1, and 3 to make a pyramid

FOURTH ROW FROM THE TOP

Cards 6 and 4

FIFTH AND FINAL ROW

Card 5

CARD POSITIONS

1 A general view of how the person sees him- or herself

2 What the person's intuition is trying to tell him or her

3 What situation needs to be nurtured now

4 The things the person has accomplished so far in life

5 The person's negative traits and beliefs

6 The person's positive traits and strengths

7 The obstacles in the way of progress

8 The person's underlying fears

9 The person's hopes and desires

SAMPLE SPIRITUAL GROWTH SPREAD

Sample question: *"I request spiritual guidance for my highest good and greatest joy."*

In this case, the first paragraph of each card's interpretation is used in the reading to correspond to each card's position.

1 A general view of how the person sees him- or herself

Ace of Cups

This is a time in your life when you are surrounded by immense happiness and creative energy. The Ace of Cups always signifies a wonderful new beginning—a period when you are eager to initiate a new project that you will truly love. Being new isn't enough to make it special—let this be something that both excites and challenges you. That way you will be motivated to follow your passion.

2 What the person's intuition is trying to tell him or her

7 The Chariot (reversed)

Even the best plans can be derailed if there are insurmountable odds blocking your progress. If that is the case, don't fool yourself by thinking that stubborn resistance alone will get you what you want. There is such a thing as being *too* focused on a plan, especially if all the indicators are showing that failure is imminent.

3 What situation needs to be nurtured now

Prince (or Knight) of Pentacles

This card suggests that hard work, sound investments, and accumulating a sizable nest egg are of singular importance to you now. If this card depicts not you but someone else, there is a chance that you work or will work with this person or may entrust him or her with a business proposition that is valuable to you. If you are the person who must conduct business with another, show that person that you have high scruples and can be trusted and relied on.

4 The things the person has accomplished so far in life

8 Strength

The key to being strong and heroic isn't that you are braver than the average human being but that you choose to go on in service to a greater cause despite your fear. There are many levels of strengths—emotional, intellectual, physical, and spiritual—and there is no telling which of these will be most useful to you at this time.

5 The person's negative traits and beliefs

Eight of Pentacles (reversed)

When it comes to an important project, you need to pay attention to everything that goes into it, taking one step at a time rather than just looking at the end result. You have the opportunity to make some additional money at this time, though you should not concentrate solely on that fact since it is likely to be a small amount. Don't be afraid that your project won't be perfect; just do the very best that you can.

6 The person's positive traits and strengths

Two of Pentacles

One of the biggest challenges in modern life is trying to juggle more than one task or one responsibility at a time. This card indicates that you will need to stay flexible while keeping informed about upcoming changes. You cannot expect things to stay the same for very long. During this period you might find yourself juggling more than one job or project, or you might have to focus on the best way to multitask in the areas of your relationships, career, and family.

7

The obstacles in the way of progress

12 The Hanged Man (reversed)

The Hanged Man reversed suggests that you not only feel stymied at this time; you may feel powerless as well. Not being able to trust your own judgment might be a problem. More than likely, you might lash out, even if you feel your self-esteem plummet, as you feel unworthy of the people and the opportunities surrounding you.

8

The person's underlying fears

4 The Emperor

This card is all about being tested and having the leadership qualities needed to stand up to such a test. This is your time to emerge as a leader; in fact, it is vital to your self-image. You will need to detach to project the proper image to others. There has probably never been a time when you were so absorbed by a desire to make goals come to fruition, and your work ethic is strong enough to make it happen. This is also a period when you could find yourself drawn to a relationship with an authority figure.

9

The person's hopes and desires

Queen of Wands (reversed)

Even if you have all the potential in the world, it won't do you any good if you don't use it correctly or to your benefit. The Queen of Wands reversed sometimes indicates that you are using your charm in a negative or cajoling way. Just because you can walk between the raindrops doesn't mean that you should. If you want to be thought of as a leader, don't make the mistake of being bossy or overly demanding. People will follow you because you inspire their respect and loyalty and not because you know what buttons to push. Behaving in such a way does a disservice to the gifts that God/Goddess has showered on you.

Tree of Life Spread

TEN CARDS

This deeply mystical spread, based on the Kabbalah and the symbolic Tree of Life, uses ten cards and highlights the wisdom we need to embrace. The Tree of Life Spread examines all of the major factors surrounding your present situation. It looks at spiritual, emotional, and physical circumstances as well as your responsibilities. It also considers obstacles and solutions.

It is a wonderfully revealing spread and is great for gaining a deeper understanding about our true nature. This type of reading can inspire us to use our unique talents to better understand ourselves and the world around us. It also can show us areas where we may need to create affirmations to deal with challenges. Leave a long time to do this reading, as it is intense.

Ask: "Give me guidance for my highest good and greatest joy."

Below are the details of the positions of this spread and their meanings.

1

YOUR HIGHEST IDEALS

This represents your soul connection to All-There-Is, the Divine. It can indicate the archetype you are most closely aligned with at present, and depicts you and your life path in the highest sense.

Kabbalah meaning: *This is where the energy of the universe enters our body, how we receive information.*

2

YOUR INTUITIVE POWER

This position indicates what you need to look at with your third eye, coming to the place where you examine your emotions and get in touch with the heart of the matter and the deeper meaning.

Kabbalah meaning: *This has to do with using metaphysical laws and spiritual principles as a guide.*

3 YOUR LOGICAL MIND

This is the position that speaks of the practical action behind the intuitive vision, the process of manifestation. It helps answer the question about the energy needed to get things activated.

Kabbalah meaning: *This has to do with common sense, rationality, and action.*

4 YOUR CREATIVE APPROACH

The deeper lessons behind your current experiences are indicated here. The qualities represented here become the mark of what you need to develop that will strengthen you and inspire others.

Kabbalah meaning: *This has to do with what your natural talents are.*

5 YOUR DAILY PRACTICE

This position represents areas where we may need to discipline ourselves, the place where we have to gain more control in order to master the qualities or situations the card refers to.

Kabbalah meaning: *This has to do with skill, force, and survival instincts.*

6 YOUR COMPASSIONATE NATURE

This represents the realms of feelings and empathy that connect your heart to the universe and those around you. It represents your sense of what you feel your mission is here, and your conscience is your guide.

Kabbalah meaning: *This is your emotional "heart" center, where you have strong desires and connections.*

7 THE LESSON LEARNED

This card speaks of the lessons that we repeat until we "graduate" from them—the habits, patterns, and events that manifest in your life that tend to be challenges. This card is a great personal empowerment card because it can also reflect the good behaviors and achievements that will repeat in our lives.

Kabbalah meaning: *This is how you can find direction and tune in to your destiny.*

8 LEVEL OF AWARENESS

This position speaks of what forces us to confront false beliefs and denial. We are made to see and take accountability for areas where we may have hypocrisy, biased opinions, and double standards.

Kabbalah meaning: *This is a motivator, how we can move forward to improve our situation.*

9 HOPES AND DREAMS

This position represents your goals and how your intentions should be focused in order to help make your dreams come true. The card in this position is a reminder of what might help or hinder your dream.

Kabbalah meaning: *This is the energy of your imagination that can help you to magnetize and manifest what you wish.*

10 MAKES YOU STRONGER

This card represents things that you do to shield and protect yourself from pain. This can also represent qualities that would be good for you to develop in an effort to make yourself stronger.

Kabbalah meaning: *This is what grounds and fortifies you physically, enabling you to have more vitality.*

SAMPLE TREE OF LIFE SPREAD

Sample question: *"Give me guidance for my highest good and greatest joy about my goal to write a book."*

In this example, we have used the "Secret" section of each card to do the reading.

1 YOUR HIGHEST IDEALS

This represents your soul connection to All-There-Is, the Divine. It can indicate the archetype you are most closely aligned with at present and depicts you and your life path in the highest sense.

Kabbalah meaning: *This is where the energy of the universe enters our body, how we receive information.*

Two of Cups

Secret: If you are not romantically involved with someone now but want to be, put your yearnings to good use by visualizing how your ideal partner will be. Feel how you will feel when the two of you are together. This is known as the Law of Attraction and acts as a magnet to attract what you visualize.

2 YOUR INTUITIVE POWER

This position indicates what you need to look at with your third eye, coming to the place where you examine your emotions and get in touch with the heart of the matter and the deeper meaning.

Kabbalah meaning: *This has to do with using metaphysical laws and spiritual principles as a guide.*

5 The Hierophant

Secret: Tradition is a wonderful thing, but it can also be an impediment to progress. Don't take a position simply because it accords with what you were taught during your formative years. Be true to what you believe now.

3 YOUR LOGICAL MIND

This is the position that speaks of the practical action behind the intuitive vision, the process of manifestation. It helps answer the question about the energy needed to get things activated.

Kabbalah meaning: *This has to do with common sense, rationality, and action.*

Four of Pentacles

Secret: At this time you could find yourself so concerned with protecting what you have that it is hard, if not impossible, to invite exciting new projects and responsibilities into your life. Keep a wise balance between the two. Don't be greedy.

4 YOUR CREATIVE APPROACH

The deeper lessons behind your current experiences are indicated here. The qualities represented here become the mark of what you need to develop that will strengthen you and inspire others.

Kabbalah meaning: *This has to do with what your natural talents are.*

Three of Cups (reversed)

Secret: Shy away from a "party person" during this period, since this individual is likely to be a superficial friend at best. He or she may bring out the shallow side of your nature or tempt you to fritter away your time. It is good to be moderate now—go the middle way.

5

YOUR DAILY PRACTICE

This position represents areas where we may need to discipline ourselves, the place where we have to gain more control in order to master the qualities or situations the card refers to.

Kabbalah meaning: *This has to do with skill, force, and survival instincts.*

17 The Star (reversed)

Secret: Even if a promising relationship beckons, you probably won't pursue it because you feel disillusioned. Cynicism and hopelessness have set in, making it hard for you to trust that renewed optimism and true love really exist.

6

YOUR COMPASSIONATE NATURE

This represents the realms of feelings and empathy that connect your heart to the universe and those around you. It represents your sense of what you feel your mission is here, and your conscience is your guide.

Kabbalah meaning: *This is your emotional "heart" center, where you have strong desires and connections.*

Seven of Swords (reversed)

Secret: Are you your own worst enemy? This is a question worth asking yourself now. Don't be afraid to stand up for yourself, but don't play a deceitful game. You should not doubt your ability to reform. Consider the vibes you are sending out to others—positive or negative?

7

THE LESSON LEARNED

This card speaks of the lessons that we repeat until we "graduate" from them—the habits, patterns, and events that manifest in your life that tend to be challenges. This card is a great personal empowerment card because it can also reflect the good behaviors and achievements that will repeat in our lives.

Kabbalah meaning: *This is how you can find direction and tune in to your destiny.*

Eight of Wands

Secret: There is such a thing as waiting too long to put plans into operation. Don't make that mistake, because the energy generated on your behalf by the universe will be this powerful for only a short time. Send a message of love!

8

LEVEL OF AWARENESS

This position speaks of what forces us to confront false beliefs and denial. We are made to see and take accountability for areas where we may have hypocrisy, biased opinions, and double standards.

Kabbalah meaning: *This is a motivator, how we can move forward to improve our situation.*

Nine of Cups

Secret: Be constantly aware of the good luck you are enjoying during this time. It is a blessed respite that can give you a sense of satisfaction and pleasure at a future time when things may not be so pleasant. Enjoy your wish!

9

HOPES AND DREAMS

This position represents your goals and how your intentions should be focused in order to help make your dreams come true. The card in this position is a reminder of what might help or hinder your dream.

Kabbalah meaning: *This is the energy of your imagination that can help you to magnetize and manifest what you wish.*

Two of Wands

Secret: Don't ignore the details of your new plans—the details are just as valuable as the bolder strokes. Keeping these two aspects of a goal in balance will ensure not only success but happiness as well. Make a list, and make a fresh start.

10

MAKES YOU STRONGER

This card represents things that you do to shield and protect yourself from pain. This can also represent qualities that would be good for you to develop in an effort to make yourself stronger.

Kabbalah meaning: *This is what grounds and fortifies you physically, enabling you to have more vitality.*

16 The Tower (reversed)

Secret: The Tower reversed could represent a sudden and much-needed break from old rules, structures, or habits that no longer serve a useful purpose in your life. This crisis could bring a sense of liberation that could propel you forward to do what needs to be done, and make a fresh start.

Magic Mandala Spread

TEN CARDS

This is a ten-card spread, which reveals a complete picture of you and the energies surrounding you. Like ***chakra****, the word* ***mandala*** *is from the classical Indian language of Sanskrit. Loosely translated to mean "circle," a mandala represents wholeness. Mandalas are sacred circles that have long been used to facilitate meditation in the Indian and Tibetan religions. Psychologist Carl Jung saw the mandala as a powerful tool toward personal understanding and growth.*

Shuffle, cut, and lay the cards out in a circle, with card 1 as the first card, at the top.

Ask: "Give me insight into my life right now" or "I seek guidance to help me on my life path."

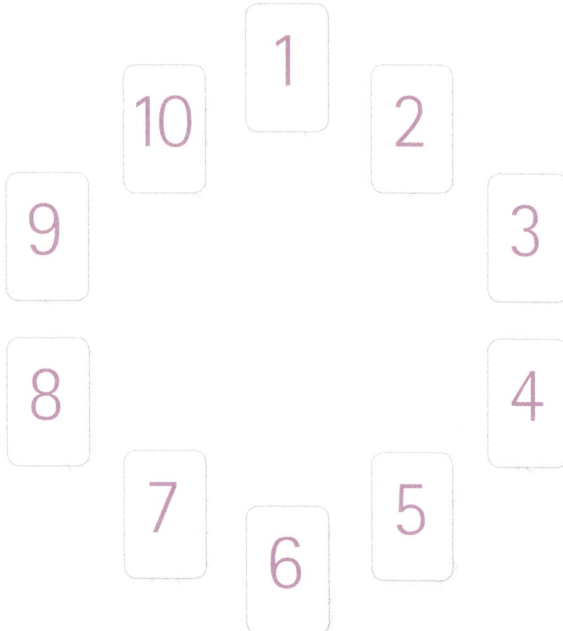

CARD POSITIONS

CARD 1
Your self-image

CARD 2
Your ambitions

CARD 3
Your spiritual ideals

CARD 4
Your accomplishments

CARD 5
Your commitments

CARD 6
Your strengths

CARD 7
Your weaknesses

CARD 8
Your secret

CARD 9
Your next step

CARD 10
Your key to open the door

SAMPLE MAGIC MANDALA SPREAD

Sample question: *"Give me insight into my life right now."*

In this example we are using the Keywords for each card to do the reading.

1 Your self-image

Six of Cups

Keywords: *Joy • Remembrance • Nostalgia • Innocence • Childhood • Pleasure*

2 Your ambitions

6 The Lovers

Keywords: *Attraction • Pact • Relationship • Choice • Attunement • Consequences*

3 Your spiritual ideals

0 The Fool

Keywords: *Trust • Innocence • Playfulness • Leisure • Adventure • Beginning*

4 Your accomplishments

Ace of Wands

Keywords: *Initiation • Breakthrough • Power • Potential • Self-confidence • Originality*

5 Your commitments

Four of Cups

Keywords: *Reevaluation • Waste • Insight • Dissatisfaction • Complaints • Regret*

6 Your strengths

Nine of Wands

Keywords: *Discipline • Guard • Preparedness • Faithfulness • Restrictions • Endurance*

7 Your weaknesses

10 The Wheel of Fortune

Keywords: *Cycles • Surprise • Timing • Karma • Fortune • Luck*

8 Your secret

Six of Pentacles

Keywords: *Generosity • Investments • Honesty • Sharing • Resources • Charity*

9 Your next step

Nine of Swords

Keywords: *Nightmare • Obsession • Anxiety • Insomnia • Dark side • Martyr*

10 Your key to open the door

Ten of Cups

Keywords: *Accomplishment • Bliss • Success • Kindness • Contentment • Respect*

Celtic Cross Spread

ELEVEN CARDS

The stone Celtic cross is the unique form of the Christian cross erected throughout Ireland and distinguished by having a circle linking the four arms of the cross as well as scenes from the Old Testament and the life of Jesus carved into the arms themselves. These crosses allowed early Christian missionaries to Ireland to use the carved scenes as visual aids in teaching scripture to the many illiterate pagans (from the Latin ***paganus****, meaning "country folk") whose ancestors had worshipped the Goddess for thousands of years. These crosses were often erected near the stone monoliths that served as places for ceremonies dedicated to the Goddess.*

The Celtic Cross Spread uses a cross whose arms are linked together by the circular development of the unfolding answer and a vertical four-card "monolith" at whose peak the ultimate outcome of the situation is found. It is ironic that the form of the Celtic Cross Spread, cross and monolith, symbolic of the supplanting of Goddess worship by Christianity, should have preserved both the memory of this event as well as the most popular form for using the Tarot, whose wisdom is descended from the former religion.

The Celtic Cross Spread should be used for the in-depth examination of a course of action. It not only predicts both the short-term and ultimate outcomes of a situation but also gives valuable insights into past conditions leading up the present time as well as comments on how hopes, fears, and the actions of others are affecting us.

After centering yourself and shuffling and cutting the deck, select eleven cards and arrange them in the following pattern.

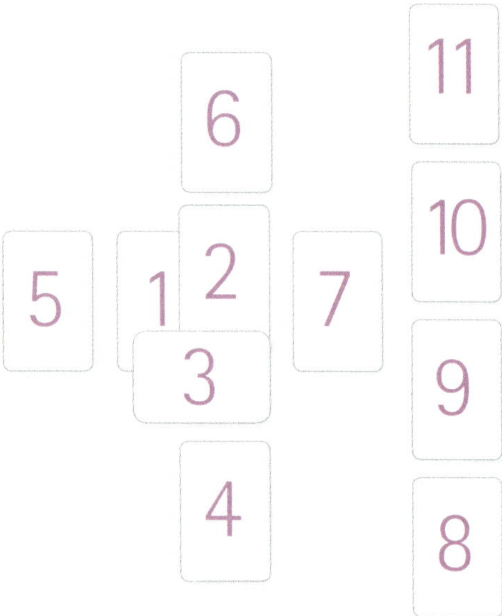

Remember, as you select each of the eleven cards for your Celtic Cross Spread, keep in mind the aspect of the situation addressed by each specific position in the spread.

1 You (also known as "the significator")

This first card represents you and your innermost desires in this situation. Some readers select this card before shuffling the Tarot deck. They pick a tarot card that exemplifies your most pressing question or your personality. It is our opinion that this practice restricts the deck from using all of its resources to give you advice about the situation. We always take the first card drawn as the significator. You must decide which method is best for you.

2 What Covers You

The second card, which is placed right on top of the first card, describes the conditions surrounding you in this situation. If the meaning of this card is conducive for the result you are desirous of achieving, then you are in a supportive atmosphere.

3 What Crosses You

The third card, which is placed across the first two cards, describes obstacles, both potential and actual, to your achieving your desires. It can represent a concept that is confusing to you or something you are not clear about. Once again, if the meaning of this card is conducive for the result you are desirous of achieving, then it is not to be viewed as negative.

4 What Is Beneath You

This card represents the basis or foundation of the situation you are inquiring about. The situation rests or turns on this factor, which can have great significance with regard to the short-term outcome. While you cannot change what the situation turns on, you can look at and, if necessary, modify your attitude toward it.

5 What Is Behind You

This card represents the past conditions and influences that have brought things to be as they are. These conditions are waning in their influence, but their memory and effect on our actions—past, present and future—must be taken into account and compensated for.

6 What Crowns You

This card represents where you would like to see this situation progress to in the future. It is the goal you should keep in sight as you work toward it. If the card in this position is a negative one, then the elimination of either that energy in your life or the quality of your reaction to that energy is a goal that must be accomplished in order for the ultimate resolution of this situation to take place.

7 What Is Before You

This card represents the short-term outcome of this situation. These are the events that will soon come to pass and must be prepared for.

8 Your Personality

This card represents how you must conduct yourself in this situation in order to achieve your desired final outcome. The appearance of a negative card in this position is a reminder that unless you conduct yourself in a way that displays your sincere desire of mastery over life's unfortunate events, you will not receive the support from other forces necessary to accomplish your mission. What course of action you take will greatly affect the final outcome.

9 How Others See You

This card represents how you are perceived in this situation. It has a strong influence on the assistance given you by your environment and the people surrounding you, such as your family, friends, co-workers, and so on. How they react to their perception of you will determine the extra energy available to you to help you meet the challenges involved with obtaining the outcome you desire. The appearance of a negative card in this position is an indication that you are going to have to rely solely on your own energies to achieve your goals. If this is the case, you must reconsider your desires. Those who would usually support you may be withholding their support because they see that your desires would not be for your ultimate good.

10 Your Hopes and Fears

This card represents your hopes or fears for the final outcome of this situation. The concept embodied in this position is a very important one because by initially considering this card as either a hope or a fear we confront the fact that what may have been holding us back from achieving our goals is not only fear of failing but the fear of how our life will be changed once we have actually reached our goal. The fear of the unknown is a basic one in all beings, yet it is imperative that this fear be overcome before any progress can be made.

11 The Final Outcome

This card represents the result of the entire course of actions taken. It is the culmination of your efforts. The appearance of a card contrary to the final outcome you desire is an indication that you must question whether what you want is good for you at this point in your development. If you decide that it still is what you desire, then you must ask for a clarification of what actions you must take in order to bring the situation to the desired conclusion. Pick an additional card to find out if you are on the right path or if the problem is one of timing.

SAMPLE CELTIC CROSS SPREAD

Sample question: *"What will be the outcome of ending my established relationship in favor of my new love interest?"*

In each position we are using the "Secret" section of the card as the answer. Be sure to interpret the card's message according the meaning of the position that it is placed in.

1 You

Queen of Wands

Secret: Use your anger as a tool, not a weapon. Instead of becoming frustrated and upset, put your emotions to good use by letting them inspire and motivate you. A good leader is a good example. Channel your energy into creative outlets.

2 What Covers You

Prince (or Knight) of Pentacles (reversed)

Secret: Be aware of the fact that if someone is cheap with money, he or she is likely to be cheap with love, too. You do not need this type of individual in your life, especially if you are an exceptionally giving person.

3 What Crosses You

Princess (or Page) of Swords

Secret: You are full of clever ideas now! Don't be too clever for your own good, though. Information should be safeguarded. Keep new theories to yourself. Write them down. Don't be tempted to gossip, even favorably. Get ready for a good surprise!

4

What Is Beneath You

Four of Pentacles (reversed)

Secret: Bear in mind the axiom "Money doesn't buy happiness." While you are right to value the resources that your enduring hard work and success have built, if you think riches alone are sufficient to bring joy, you are mistaken. Those who are cheap with money are cheap with love.

5

What Is Behind You

19 The Sun

Secret: Happiness and a love of life are in the air. Your natural charm and charisma have a strong effect on others now. There could be a wonderful new relationship on the horizon. Home and family situations are sunny and bright. Let your light shine.

6

What Crowns You

I The Magician

Secret: Use your skill and intelligence to create a more brilliant reality for yourself. Truly, the sky is the limit. By channeling the positive energy of the universe and visualizing what you would like to see happen, you can manifest and enrich your future. Pretend that you are a magician asking the universe for what you want and expecting it to deliver right on time!

7

What Is Before You

Princess (or Page) of Cups

Secret: Your current situation is not unlike being pregnant—you need to give birth to tender feelings, bringing them into a loving world where they are prized, needed, and wanted. You are their "mother" and will continue to tend them. Listen to your dreams. Be gentle.

8

Your Personality

13 Death

Secret: It is time to come to terms with a new reality. That doesn't mean that old habits or beliefs were wrong—they have simply worn out their welcome. Once you realize that you can find fulfillment in your new life, you will be less likely to stay with the status quo and more curious about what is coming your way.

9

How Others See You

Five of Pentacles (reversed)

Secret: Beware of your current level of anxiety. You may be experiencing actual panic attacks, which is a condition that requires treatment. Seek professional help for frightening, conflicting feelings and emotional upheavals that you may experience.

10

Your Hopes and Fears

Two of Wands (reversed)

Secret: Things are in flux; you should not attempt to make too many plans for the future at this time. Let one change lead naturally to the next, rather than trying to make things happen according to plan. You'll regret it if you do.

11

The Final Outcome

Ace of Cups

Secret: Joy, health, happiness, and excitement are being offered to you on the proverbial silver platter. Don't ignore these gifts of love or allow them to go unappreciated. Allow yourself to feel the positive benefits flowing into and out of your heart.

Zodiac Wheel Spread

TWELVE CARDS

This twelve-card spread identifies the twelve most important issues affecting the twelve most important areas of one's life at the present moment and how to make the most of them. The strength of this spread is that it provides information about all areas of a person's life.

It describes what is in store in the twelve major areas of life for the coming year or whatever time frame one puts into the question, such as "Describe what I should focus on in the important areas of my life for the next six-month period."

The twelve cards represent the twelve zodiac houses: Personality, Resources, Communications, Home, Creativity, Health, Partnership, Mysteries, Philosophy, Career, Friends, and Limitations.

When a card is interpreted, it is done so in the meaning of the house the card is placed in.

To lay down the spread, place the first card in the nine o'clock position. Then lay the rest of the cards counterclockwise.

Card 1 relates to the First House of Personality; card 2 to the Second House of Material Resources, and so on. The meanings of the Twelve Houses are as follows:

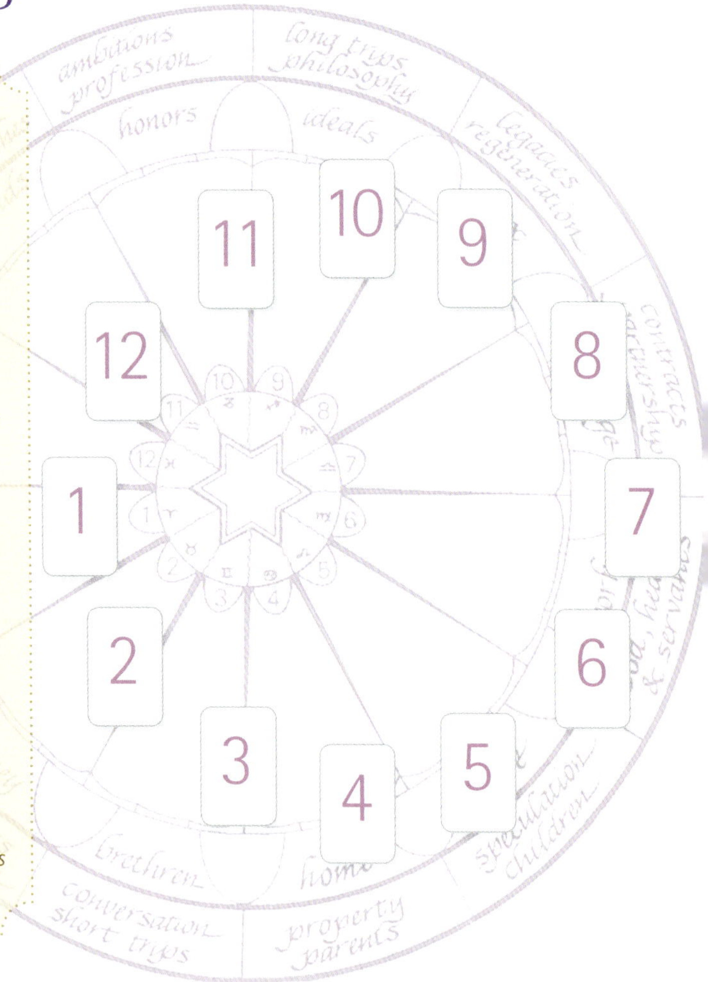

TWELVE HOUSES OF THE ZODIAC

1 FIRST HOUSE OF PERSONALITY

Describes my outlook on life and how I present myself. How do others see me?

2 SECOND HOUSE OF MATERIAL RESOURCES

Finances, possessions, values. How can I improve my finances?

3 THIRD HOUSE OF COMMUNICATIONS

Communications, immediate environment, brothers and sisters, short trips. How can I make connections?

4 FOURTH HOUSE OF THE HOME

Home environment, the mother, ending cycles. How can I best deal with my past?

5 FIFTH HOUSE OF CREATIVITY

Self-expression, children, love affairs, speculation. How can I express my creativity?

6 SIXTH HOUSE OF HEALTH

Work and service, physical and mental well-being, job, community endeavors, pets. How can I improve my work and career?

7 SEVENTH HOUSE OF PARTNERS

Partnerships, both marital and business. How can I improve my relationships?

8 EIGHTH HOUSE OF MYSTERIES

Mysteries in life, regenerating influences, legacies. How can I make big changes?

9 NINTH HOUSE OF PHILOSOPHY

State of mind, travel, studies, philosophy. How can I feed my soul?

10 TENTH HOUSE OF CAREER

Occupation, status, the father. How can I become more successful?

11 ELEVENTH HOUSE OF FRIENDS, HOPES, AND WISHES

Favorable influences and trends. How can I make my dreams real?

12 TWELFTH HOUSE OF LIMITATIONS

Limiting influences and karma. What's blocking me?

SAMPLE ZODIAC WHEEL SPREAD

Sample question: *"Describe what I should focus on to improve my life for the next four-month period."*

Start the reading by interpreting the card in the First House, and continue in sequence until all twelve houses have been read and interpreted.

In this example we are using the "Quick Read" section of each card interpretation for each of the card spread positions to do the reading.

1 FIRST HOUSE OF PERSONALITY

Describes my outlook on life and how I present myself. How do others see me?

Seven of Wands

Quick Read: *Defend your beliefs.*

2 SECOND HOUSE OF MATERIAL RESOURCES

Finances, possessions, values. How can I improve my finances?

Ten of Swords (reversed)

Quick Read: *Seek help for your problems.*

3 THIRD HOUSE OF COMMUNICATIONS

Communications, immediate environment, brothers and sisters, short trips. How can I make connections?

Four of Pentacles

Quick Read: *Hold on to what you have.*

4 FOURTH HOUSE OF THE HOME

Home environment, the mother, ending cycles. How can I best deal with my past?

15 The Devil (reversed)

Quick Read: *Wear a mask.*

5 FIFTH HOUSE OF CREATIVITY

Self-expression, children, love affairs, speculation. How can I express my creativity?

Queen of Swords (reversed)

Quick Read: *Be strong, but not too strong!*

6 SIXTH HOUSE OF HEALTH

Work and service, physical and mental well-being, job, community endeavors, pets. How can I improve my work and career?

Two of Wands

Quick Read: *Make a plan.*

7 SEVENTH HOUSE OF PARTNERS

Partnerships, both marital and business. How can I improve my relationships?

Eight of Cups (reversed)

Quick Read: *Don't be too self-sacrificing.*

8 EIGHTH HOUSE OF MYSTERIES

Mysteries in life, regenerating influences, legacies. How can I make big changes?

Five of Swords

Quick Read: *Learn from your mistakes.*

9 NINTH HOUSE OF PHILOSOPHY

State of mind, travel, studies, philosophy. How can I feed my soul?

7 The Chariot

Quick Read: *Listen to your head, not your heart.*

10 TENTH HOUSE OF CAREER

Occupation, status, the father. How can I become more successful?

Princess (or Page) of Wands (reversed)

Quick Read: *Act your age.*

11 ELEVENTH HOUSE OF FRIENDS, HOPES, AND WISHES

Favorable influences and trends. How can I make my dreams real?

18 The Moon

Quick Read: *Journey through the unknown.*

12 TWELFTH HOUSE OF LIMITATIONS

Limiting influences and karma. What's blocking me?

13 Death (reversed)

Quick Read: *Resistance is futile.*

The Secret Origin of the Tarot

Today when people think about predicting the future, they usually don't realize how seriously this subject used to be taken. They don't think about the Oracle at Delphi, where wars were started, stopped, and averted. They forget the prophets and prophecies of the Bible or that Jesus was the fulfillment of a prophecy. They forget that the Prophet is the most honored title of Islam's Muhammad.

Like most people who've become successful, religions are somewhat uncomfortable about their roots, and so they want to relegate the foretelling of the future to their own specially chosen people of the distant past and cast doubt and downright animosity on anyone who might claim to have that ability now. This is why personal prophecy, which is how Amy and I think of our lifelong study of Tarot card reading, has been put down for centuries as mere fortune-telling.

There is an old joke told about every kind of scholar: Put two of them in a room and you will get three opinions; it is the same with Tarot historians. Some say the Tarot started out as pasteboard pictures of various gods and goddesses used to teach their divine properties to the illiterate and brought to Europe by travelers from India. These travelers arrived when all things Egypt were the rage and found it advantageous to be known as "Gyptees." Their descendents are now known as Gypsies.

That theory might account for many people believing the Tarot originated in Egypt. However, there are those who claim that the Tarot came from tenth-century China, and there are advocates for Hebraic, Islamic, and Indian origins as well. One thing seems certain: The earliest and most complete deck of Tarot cards dates from the early fifteenth century and is said to have been made for the Duke of Milan.

Egypt advocates say Tarot derives from the words *tar* and *ro*, meaning the "royal road." Indian advocates like to remind everyone that the word *taru* means "cards" in Hindu and that Tara is the Aryan name for the Great Mother Goddess. Those voting for Tarot being a product of the Hebrew culture point to the word Torah, their name for the first five books of the Bible. However, remember that one of the areas where the cards first appeared was Milan, in northern Italy, where there is a river called the Taro.

There is evidence that the first Tarot decks were as likely to have been used as a card game as for divinatory guidance. There is probably more than a little truth in that. There is a French word, *tares*, that is used to describe the small dot border on playing cards. You can, however, do readings with ordinary playing cards—many professional readers do it that way. So even if Tarot cards were originally a gaming deck, that doesn't mean they were not used for divination.

Even the date of the first true Tarot deck is in dispute. The oldest surviving Tarot cards are from fifteen fragmented decks painted in the fifteenth century for the Visconti-Sforza family, the rulers of Milan. You can buy a reproduction of this historic deck, though it is a bit pricey.

We believe that Tarot cards have had an important though often unacknowledged influence on events for centuries. It is said that when Napoleon's wife, the empress Josephine, was a young woman living quietly in a small village, she consulted a card reader. The Tarot reader laid her cards on the table and predicted remarkable things: This unknown girl was to become the first lady of France and the most prominent woman of her time.

In our time, we have seen Tarot readings reflect and predict important events for us and those we read for. We have been told by our friends who are professional readers that they, too, have had the same experience with their clients.

Whatever its origin, the Tarot came a long way in the twentieth century. The wisdom of the cards was an irresistible target for great artists, once they no longer were afraid of the persecution and ridicule that surrounded them up until the revolutionary times of the 1960s.

The Tarot attracted both famous artists, such as surrealist Salvador Dalí, and those undeservedly not so well-known, such as Pamela Coleman Smith, who under the vigilant eye of Arthur Edward Waite created in 1909 what we now know as the Rider-Waite deck, the most famous Tarot deck of the twentieth century.

Interest in the Tarot has continued to grow in the last few decades and shows no sign of subsiding. We believe that artists will continue to create many different new Tarot decks to reflect the various new perspectives of the twenty-first century. One thing is certain: The Tarot, like the images that we see in our dreams, can bring us messages of great importance and is a powerful tool that guides us, opens doors, and unlocks secrets.

The Secret of Why the Tarot Works

The nearest thing to an explanation of why the Tarot works is an ancient theory held by many peoples throughout the world and rediscovered in the twentieth century by the pioneering Swiss psychologist Carl Jung (1875–1961). He seems to have understood the symbolic importance of the images of the Tarot, regarding the cards as representing archetypes of people or conditions, universal symbols rooted in our subconscious. The Emperor, for instance, represents the ultimate patriarchal figure. Jung actually had a reason for why shuffling a card deck while asking a question could produce a decipherable answer.

His theory of synchronicity (from the Greek *syn* meaning "together" and *chronos* meaning "time") proposed that events happening at the same moment had a relationship of significance. In other words, when you ask your question with sincerity and you intend to get an answer, you will get an answer, possibly in many ways. It depends on how good you are at deciphering the events around you at the moment you ask the question. A flock of birds, cloud formations, or the pattern the wind makes in the trees all could hold the answer. The Tarot is a sort of sacred machine devised to respond to your question and freeze your answer as a picture in time so that you may decipher it.

The Spiritual Journey Through the Major Arcana

The spiritual journey of the twenty-two cards of the Major Arcana, or "greater secrets," of the Tarot can be viewed as an allegory for the great quest for self-knowledge and growth taken by each soul as it plays its part in the drama that is life on earth. It is a story told by the meanings of the symbolic images of the Major Arcana as well as by the numerical position assigned to each of them. They tell the story of the development of The Fool's journey, filled with lessons of life, success to be achieved, goals to be reached, and obstacles to be dealt with.

The first person we meet on our journey is The Fool. His number is zero because he represents the unborn soul before it takes its first step into the physical world. Aware of his eternal unity with the divine in all things, he has no fear as he takes a giant step into a new life and all it will bring.

Next we meet The Magician, whose understanding of and mastery over the four elements of reality, fire (action), air (ideas), water (emotion), and earth (matter), symbolized by the Wands (also called Clubs, Scepters, Rods, or Roses), Swords (also called Spades, Blades, or Wings), Cups (also called Hearts, Chalices, or Shells), and Pentacles (also called Diamonds, Coins, or Gems), the suits of the Minor Arcana, will enable him to work his will on his world. His number is one because he symbolizes the individual's first awareness of his or her own power and place in a world that is the individual's to use.

Encountering The High Priestess in her moonlit grotto, we are reminded that there is a power beyond that of the visible world. The High Priestess has no need of thoughts, words, or actions. She knows all because she is aware of the connectedness of all things. Her number, two, is a sign that there are two different types of skills necessary to really make magic. The active, physical, and verbal skills of The Magician must be developed and blended with the passive, emotional, and intuitive ways of The High Priestess in order for us to prepare ourselves for the encounters ahead.

The number of our next host on the spiritual journey, the pregnant Empress, is three. The Empress, like her child, is symbolic of the new life resulting from the harmonious blending of the purely male energies of The Magician and the purely female energies of The High Priestess. The Empress gives birth to the natural world that surrounds and nourishes us.

Her husband, The Emperor, whose number is four, commands the four corners of the world brought into being by his Empress. He represents our desire to dominate not only the four elements of our own lives but those of the lives of others as well.

When we meet The Hierophant, we meet a man who has gone beyond trying to control the world of the four elements through physical means. He has established order in the world through moral authority, representing the One Spirit that pervades all, the fifth element of life's mixture. But his number, five, is also a reminder that, like the five-pointed star—the universal symbol for a human being, taken from the outline of our head, arms, and legs—this holy man is nothing more or less than a man.

The problem of being just a man or a just man is encountered when we go beyond the rules of The Hierophant and enter the realm of The Lovers, which is ruled by the heart. Here we have the eternal dilemma of having to make choices based on the dictates of our free will and not on mores and guidelines handed down to us from the ages. The number of The Lovers, six, is a reference to the two choices available to each of the three participants in this scene. It is also symbolic of the six directions—forward, backward, left, right, up, and down—available to each of us at all times.

When we ride along with The Chariot, we learn that we have no choice but to take only the actions that will be in our best interest. To win a race we must sometimes even ride alone. Seven, the number of The Chariot, corresponds to the seven chakras, the energy centers running from the base of the spine up to the top of the head. They are the intake and outflow points of the astral (of the stars) energy, which feeds and nourishes the various levels of our being and makes all our actions on the physical, mental, and emotional levels possible.

When we arrive at the dramatic scene depicted in Strength, we are confronted with the fact that to really succeed in life we are going to have to harmonize our desires with those of the natural world we share. Unless we are gently but precisely balanced between the world of spirit and the here and now, knowing without a shadow of a doubt that we are one with all, we will be symbolically torn to pieces, in this case by the lioness shown on the tarot card, trapped by our handiwork, whose natural instincts can sense our hesitancy and fear. Eight, the number of Strength, is seen here as the universal symbol for infinity, floating above the spiritual energy center at the top of the head of the beautiful young princess. It tells us that she has passed her test and is indeed connected to the infinite source of all creation.

We meet The Hermit walking the path of knowledge he has followed for many years since he passed his own test of strength. This master has withdrawn from the world so that those who seek to share his wisdom will have to prove their sincerity by making the effort to find him. His number is nine because nine, when added to any other number, will give as a sum a number whose component numbers, added together as individual numbers, will add up to the number that was originally added to nine, for example, $1 + 9 = 10 = 1 + 0 = 1$; $2 + 9 = 11 = 1 + 1 = 2$; $3 + 9 = 12 = 1 + 2 = 3$; and so on. (If you have the time and the knowledge-seeking inclination of The Hermit, you may try it with any number—it always works.)

When we journey with The Hermit for a while on the path to enlightenment and incorporate his wisdom into our lives, we come to realize that it is our true selves that he has enabled us to be more in contact with. The purpose of our walk with The Hermit and the entire spiritual journey is to bring us home to our Higher Self, the observer and true participant in all our diverse lifetimes.

The wise Hermit can give us the impression that our world is completely knowable. When we come to the place of The Wheel of Fortune, however, we learn that sometimes wisdom and strength do not enable us to understand or change our luck. The wheel is the ancient symbol of the idea that everything comes to pass in its appointed time and season. The number of The Wheel of Fortune is ten ($10 = 1 + 0 = 1$), a reference to the fact that the number ten begins the cycle of numbers again. Reducing the number ten to its component numbers gives us the number one, symbolic of our encounter with the vaguely human face of a sphinx, who silently reminds us that we each must confront the up-and-down cycles of our lives alone.

The welcome face of the angel of Justice meets us at our next stop on the spiritual journey. Her perfectly balanced scales are a message that although we have assigned the apparently random occurrences in our lives to dumb luck, they are actually physical manifestations of Justice working in our own lives. Eleven ($11 = 1 + 1 = 2$), the number of Justice, is symbolic of the two pans of the scale she holds. The balancing of the scales, one plus one, yields two, the number of relationships. Without Justice neither relationships nor society is possible.

When we come upon The Hanged Man, it seems we have met a victim of Justice. The role of Justice, however, is not to inflict pain but to bring to us the experiences we need in order to balance out the excesses of personality that are blocking our spiritual development. The Hanged Man is suspended in order that he may reconsider his actions from a new perspective. His number, twelve

(12 = 1 + 2 = 3), is the number of the months of the year and the signs of the astrological zodiac. These divisions of time are used to bring order to the people of the world symbolized by The Magician (1) and The High Priestess (2) as well as to the other growing things of the world symbolized by The Empress (3). Do not worry about The Hanged Man; the wait will do him some good.

Our encounter with Death can symbolize that we have learned our lessons so well that we are no longer the same person. Thirteen, which has gotten a bad reputation from its long association with the card of Death, is the age when a child becomes an adult, sexually speaking. Most religions have ceremonies marking this time of the "death" of the child. If we fear death, we can never grow beyond the fears of childhood or go further on our spiritual journey, because to fear death is to fear life. The component numbers of thirteen (13 = 1 + 3 = 4) tell us that death can come to our energetic manipulation of the physical elements represented by The Magician (1), to all growing things on earth given birth to by The Empress (3), as well as to all rulers of the world who are under the authority of The Emperor (4), but never to our nonphysical, emotional, and intuitive being symbolized by The High Priestess (2), the number missing from Death's equation.

The addition of our symbolic encounter with Death to the list of places we have visited is not to be taken lightly. While an essential part of our journey, this experience can be so overwhelming that we must immediately be reminded that it is only one stop on a long voyage. Our visit with the angelic teacher and serene student of the card Temperance is a time for healing. Here we can learn that we have ample time to mix all the knowledge we can accumulate of the physical world with faith in our divine nature to give us a rich and rewarding life.

Fourteen (14 = 1 + 4 = 5), the number of Temperance, is a reminder that our bodies are made of the elements that The Magician (1) and The Emperor (4) use and command, but our essential nature is that of the fifth element of the One Soul, whose representative on earth we have met in the form of The Hierophant (5). Like Temperance, he also wanted to comfort us as best as he knew how in the face of both Death and the host of our next stop on the spiritual journey, The Devil.

The Devil can twist the words of all the lessons we have learned and trick us into believing that they are as much lies as what he is telling us. He can convince us that the quickest way to gain all that we desire is through deceit and trickery. But he can harm us only if we are blind to the fact that only we have the power to choose order over chaos and a life spent making our world better instead of trying to take as much as we can to our grave. The number of The Devil, fifteen (15 = 1 + 5 = 6), is a reminder of our meeting with The Lovers (6). It was there where The Magician's individuality (1) was confronted by the morality of The Hierophant (5) and we first encountered the bittersweet aspects of choice, a part of the free will that is our birthright.

Let's pass quickly by The Tower lest we be struck by lightning or by the debris falling from this once-proud edifice. The number of The Tower, sixteen (16 = 1 + 6 = 7), is a clue that we are witnessing the downfall of The Magician (1), who thought his handiwork could last forever; The Lovers (6), who gave up on the journey and tried to build their world based only on physical love and not spiritual development; and the proud, confident, and self-absorbed heroine of The Chariot (7), who built a monument to her glory but failed to learn that pride comes before a fall. This lesson can be painful even if it is not a physical pain that must be endured.

The explosive destruction of The Tower has cleared the land and the air of the stagnation that power too long entrenched can bring. A new order must be built on a foundation of higher knowledge, not merely on stone. The number of The Star, seventeen (17 = 1 + 7 = 8), recalls the enduring Strength (8) we can achieve by blending our desires with those of a higher, natural order. This is the proper use of the material talents of The Magician (1) in combination with the heroism and the astral energy centers of The Chariot (7). By making beautiful art out of every breath of our life through inspiration (literally the breathing in of the spirit), we can both make lasting structures and heal ourselves after the upheaval we have suffered at The Tower. But what The Star wants us to take with us when we leave her is the knowledge that strength of an even greater value can be ours if we cleanse ourselves of all desires.

Traditionally, our sojourn in the land of The Moon was considered the most frightening. This may be because The Moon had been the symbol of the Goddess, the female deity who was worshipped as the Supreme Being for thousands of years until the male-dominated religions of the last two thousand years challenged her supremacy. Their typical male competitiveness compelled them to use every method, from the incorporation of her customs and rituals at the beginning of the present era to the violence and persecutions of the Inquisition (1200s to 1800s), to ensure that patriarchal religions would succeed and overcome the matriarchal religions and some of their barbaric excesses.

There is much evidence that the Tarot itself was a barely tolerated refuge for the higher concepts associated with worship of the Goddess, allowed to exist only because it was considered merely an amusement. Little wonder then that The Moon, universal symbol of the Goddess, would be assigned the unpopular meaning of a terrifying journey. Our deck *The Enchanted Tarot* has tried to restore The Moon to its rightful meaning of trust in the protection afforded us by an energy watching over us. The Moon challenges us to have faith and go on even in the pitch black that comes just before the dawn.

Like The Hermit (9), The Moon, number eighteen (18 = 1 + 8 = 9), is a solitary being dwelling in darkness, whose compassion, wisdom, and light are there to lead us home to our Higher Self. Like all of us, our old friend The Magician (1), representing the individual, must ally himself with true Strength (8) in order to pass through this "dark night of the soul" and attain the wisdom possessed by The Hermit (9).

The formless shapes and nameless terrors of our dark side must be conquered before we can bask in the glorious life-giving rays of The Sun. The Sun's number, nineteen (19 = 1 + 9 = 10 = 1 + 0 = 1), is symbolic of its supreme creative ability. Taking the manipulative powers of The Magician (1) and combining them with the natural wisdom of The Hermit (9), then adding the divinely guided luck of The Wheel of Fortune (10) and the fearless trust and awareness of divine unity possessed by The Fool (0), gives us a power that brings both life and light to the world.

There is a strong temptation to linger in the land of The Sun, but by this time on our journey we know that we must always keep moving forward.

Flying over the tall peaks, we meet the angelic herald of Judgment, whose horn announces a call to purify ourselves in preparation for the end of our spiritual journey. We have come far and seen and learned much. But the number of Judgment, twenty (20 = 2 + 0 = 2), is a message that unless we apply, not only in our own lives but in our dealings with all, the order, peace, and balance learned from Justice (11 = 1 + 1 = 2) and the compassionate knowledge that is beyond language, symbolized by the all-knowing High Priestess (2), we will never reach our full potential.

And so we finally are ready to come to The World. We are here to learn about ourselves and the world that is a reflection of ourselves. Our higher purpose, though, is to assist in the co-creation of the world by using our knowledge to help all. By uniting the feminine principles symbolized by The High Priestess (2) and the masculine principles symbolized by The Magician (1)—in that order—we finally gain The World (21 = 2 + 1 = 3) and get to dance in the enjoyment of its fertile, abundant beauty, which The Empress (3), twin sister of The High Priestess, knew about all along.

The spiritual journey, like The World, has no real beginning and no real end. It is a never-ending cycle that spirals around and up and down but always leads us back to ourselves and the realization that life is movement, change, awareness, and growth. There is always more of ourselves to learn from and learn about.

ABOUT THE AUTHORS
Monte Farber & Amy Zerner

Internationally known self-help author Monte Farber's inspiring guidance and empathic insights impact everyone he encounters. Amy Zerner's exquisite, one-of-a-kind spiritual couture creations and collaged fabric paintings exude her profound intuition and deep connection with archetypal stories and healing energies. For more than thirty years they've combined their deep love for each other with the work of inner exploration and self-discovery to build The Enchanted World of Amy Zerner and Monte Farber: books, card decks, and oracles that have helped millions answer questions, find deeper meaning, and follow their own spiritual paths.

Together they've made their love for each other a work of art and their art the work of their lives. Their best-selling titles include *The Chakra Meditation Kit, The Tarot Discovery Kit, Karma Cards, The Enchanted Spellboard, Secrets of the Fortune Bell, Little Reminders: Love & Relationships, Little Reminders: The Law of Attraction, Goddess, Guide Me!, The Animal Powers Meditation Kit, Astrology Gems, True Love Tarot, The Enchanted Tarot, The Instant Tarot Reader, The Psychic Circle, Wish upon a Star, The Pathfinder Psychic Talking Board, The Truth Fairy, Spirit of the Ancestors Altar Kit, Vibe-Away!, The Mystic Messenger, The Breathe Easy Deck, The Healing Deck,* and *The Ghostwriter Automatic Writing Kit.*

Visit their popular website:
www.TheEnchantedWorld.com

Or write to them at:
The Enchanted World
Box 2299
East Hampton, NY
USA 11937